BREEDING
CONURES

Sun Conures, *Aratinga solstitialis*, adult pair.

BREEDING CONURES

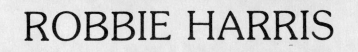

ROBBIE HARRIS

This book is dedicated to the most wonderful person in the world, my grandmother Lena Share.

ISBN 0-87666-870-8

Distributed in the UNITED STATES by T.F.H. Publications, Inc., 211 West Sylvania Avenue, Neptune City, NJ 07753; in CANADA by Rolf C. Hagen Ltd., 3225 Sartelon Street, Montreal 382 Quebec; in ENGLAND by T.F.H. (Great Britain) Ltd., 11 Ormside Way, Holmethorpe Industrial Estate, Redhill, Surrey RH1 2PX; in AUSTRALIA AND THE SOUTH PACIFIC by Pet Imports Pty. Ltd., Box 149 Brookvale 2100 N.S.W., Australia; in SOUTH AFRICA by Multipet (Pty.) Ltd., 30 Turners Avenue, Durban 4001. Published by T.F.H. Publications Inc. Ltd., The British Crown Colony of Hong Kong.

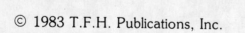

Photographs by Fred Harris

Right: "Nansun" Conure hen, determined by surgical sexing. This interspecific hybrid (Nanday x Sun), one of a brood of three, is one year old.

Facing page, top: White-eyed Conure, *Aratinga leucophthalmus,* adult hen. *Bottom:* Mitred Conure, *Aratinga mitrata,* adult.

Slender-billed Conure,
*Enicognathus
leptorhynchus*, adult male.

Sun Conure, *Aratinga
solstitialis*, adult male.

Contents

Acknowledgments

This book would have never been possible without my husband Fred, who always urged keeping and breeding conures of all kinds, long before we ever owned any. I want to thank him for all the time he spent taking so many beautiful photos for this book. His love for conures and interest in them are superb.

I would also like to thank Tony Silva of Illinois and my Australian friend John Zitta, who encouraged me all through the writing of this book.

To our veterinarians, Max E. Weiss and Hannis L. Stoddard III, I would like to express my gratitude for their conscientious help and all the work they've done on our birds.

A special thanks to Frank Lanier of West Hollywood, California, for keeping his eyes open and helping us acquire a great many of our birds.

And last, but never least, many thanks to my parents, family, and friends for their helpfulness and understanding when it comes to my birds.

Top: Red-fronted Conure *Aratinga wagleri frontata,* adult male. *Bottom:* Red-masked Conure, *Aratinga erythrogenys,* adult male.

8

Introduction

Conures, in my opinion, are the up-and-coming birds of the future. They are becoming more and more popular. For years people have been raising the bread-and-butter birds (budgies, lovebirds, and Cockatiels) and have never ventured into the world of conures. Now that conures are becoming better known as pets, the average aviculturist is starting to pair up and breed many species of conures. Obtained at a young age or hand-raised, conures make excellent pets and are very intelligent and affectionate toward their owners.

Conures come in numerous colors from brown to bright green, red, orange, blue, and yellow. They range in size from eight inches to twenty inches and have a slender shape and a long tapered tail. When conures are properly taken care of, they will breed easily and be very prolific. They usually make excellent parents, and once they start to breed, they will continue for many years to raise babies. Conures are also very hardy birds—here in southern California, ours are kept outdoors all year long.

For the past eleven years, my husband and I have owned and bred many different species of birds. We, too, started with budgies, Cockatiels, and lovebirds. About two years ago, we ventured into other kinds of parrots. Our collection of conures, which keeps growing, now consists of Suns, Jandayas, Cactuses, Brown-throats, Golden-caps, Nandays, Peach-fronts, Mitreds, Red-masks, Blue-crowns, Duskies, Patagonians, Maroon-bellies, Green-cheeks, Painteds, and Green conures. We also have rosellas, caiques, cockatoos, macaws, Barred and Andean parakeets, kakarikis, many other kinds of parrots, and a large variety of lovebirds and Cockatiels. We have raised many chicks from the many pairs of birds that we own and breed. All our babies are hand-reared; there have been many occasions when I have been hand-feeding over eighty baby chicks of all kinds.

This book deals mostly with the *breeding* of conures. Everything explained in this book is based on our own experiences in keeping and raising conures. I am not saying that our way is right; nor am I saying that someone else is doing it wrong! Everything in here works for us, but as you start to keep and breed conures, you will develop some of your own techniques. I wish everybody breeding conures lots of luck and lots of babies!

Painted Conures, *Pyrrhura picta*, adult pair.

Selecting a Conure

Before You Purchase It is very important that you give a new bird a physical examination before you purchase it. The examination should include the body, eyes, head, face, nostrils, cere, mouth, beak, feathers, skin, feet, and legs.

You should observe the bird's behavior closely while it is still in the cage or aviary—try to purchase one that is not too nervous. I own a conure that was once very high-strung and would rub her head up and down the cage bars until all of her head feathers and some skin were scraped off. Some high-strung birds do calm down and will go to nest when given a mate, as mine did, but there are a few that are always moving and nervous and may never settle down to breed. Also, see that the bird holds itself proudly and is not droopy. Check the wing carriage to make sure they are held neatly folded. If one wing hangs down, it may mean that at one time the wing was broken and did not heal properly. The bird may not be able to fly, which means it couldn't be kept in an aviary. Any conure that cannot fly should be kept only in a cage, for if the bird is placed in an aviary, a fall from the top might prove fatal.

Try to check the bird's droppings in the cage where the bird has been kept to see if they are too watery. Very watery droppings may mean the bird is sick. Once the bird is moved into a new cage, the droppings may be watery for a while because the bird is nervous.

The eyes of almost any bird say quite a lot. They should look bright and clear, not tearing, sleepy-looking, or swollen. When you approach the cage, the bird should be very alert.

The feathers should look strong and shiny. There should be no bare patches or gray down covering the bird, which could mean a vitamin deficiency or that the bird is a self-plucker. If the bird plucks its own feathers, there is a very good chance the bird will still breed; but it may start plucking its mate or their babies, sometimes even killing the offspring.

Birds coming out of quarantine have gone through an awful lot. Most of them have ragged and rough-looking feathers. They are missing feathers from being plucked by other birds or fighting. This condition is usually temporary. The damaged feathers will molt out after a few months, with the bird probably looking as good as new. I will admit that I myself

11

have purchased birds in very bad feather condition, but with a proper diet, their plumage has almost always returned to normal.

The bird should appear well balanced, with strong feet that grasp the perch securely. Check the feet and legs of the bird to see that they are free of any abscess and that the bird does not limp from an old or recent injury. For breeding, it is very important that the male have good, strong feet and most claws, if not all, to be able to hold onto the hen.

The bird's cere should be clean, not wet or dirty from runny nostrils, which could mean a cold, or worse. Check for wheezing or rattling breath sounds, since these indicate an illness. The beak should look strong and solid, but some natural wear is all right. If the mandibles are crossed or overgrown, the bird's beak will probably have to be trimmed periodically.

Part the feathers to check the bird's skin. It should look clean, not flaky or peeling. Avoid any birds with wartlike lesions, scabs, or swollen joints, which could mean an infection or pox. It is also very important that the overall look of the bird is solid, with no sharp breastbone. Feel the breast to be sure it is firmly fleshed. The vent feathers should be clean, not soiled with droppings—another sign of illness.

The main point in selecting a good, healthy bird is to use your good judgment. Please don't buy just any bird; look the bird over carefully and make sure it appears healthy. The best thing in selecting any bird is to use common sense.

Nanday Conures in a holding pen, shortly after release from quarantine.

Green-winged Macaw, *Ara chloroptera.* This hen was a very tame pet until we purchased a tame male and set them up for breeding. Now, being unafraid of humans, both will attack if you enter their flight.

It's commonplace to hear that conures resemble macaws. A Blue-fronted Amazon, *Amazona aestiva*, beside a Finsch's Conure, *Aratinga finschi*, permits a comparison between aratingas and amazons.

Mitred Conure, *Aratinga mitrata*, adult. Largest of the aratingas, the Mitred is bigger than some species of amazons.

Golden-capped Conure, *Aratinga auricapilla*, adult hen. This conure is closely related, everyone agrees, to the Sun and Jandaya conures.

Red-fronted Conure
Aratinga wagleri frontata,
adult male.

Kinds of Conures Conures come in many sizes and colors. The *Aratinga* conures are more readily available than other species. The aratingas are found from Mexico and the Caribbean Islands through Central and most of South America. In size they range from the small Orange-fronted Conure, which is about nine inches long, to the large Mitred Conure, with a total length of fifteen inches. Members of the genus *Aratinga* resemble the macaws, in miniature. They make excellent and very affectionate pets, especially the hand-fed, tame babies. They can be taught to do tricks and can also learn to talk. The only problem with most of the aratingas is that they have very loud voices. One kept by itself as a pet is usually fairly quiet, but with neighbors close by, it would be difficult to keep many. We have some conures that love to vocalize all day; on the other hand, one pair of our Sun Conures are very quiet, and you never hear them. Without a doubt, each conure has its own personality; all are individuals, so I cannot say that all conures are loud. You will find that every pair of conures is different. I have found that when conures are on eggs or chicks, they are usually very quiet. The following are some of the most widely available *Aratinga* conures:

The Sun Conure (*Aratinga solstitialis*) is one of the most beautiful conures, besides being an excellent breeder. Bright gold and orange dominate their coloring, and in some birds the orange approaches a vivid red-orange. The wings and tail feathers show blue and green. The beak and feet are black. Immature birds have less golden color and are mostly green, resembling the Jandaya Conure. The overall length is twelve inches.

The Jandaya Conure (*Aratinga jandaya*) resembles the Sun Conure, but with more green plumage. The head is a bright yellow, which gradually changes on the throat and neck to the bright red of the breast. The rump and under-wings are a bright red-orange. The back is green, and the wings and tail show both blue and green. The beak and feet are black. Most immature birds have green flecks on their yellow heads and are not as brightly colored as the adults. The length is twelve inches.

The Golden-Capped Conure (*Aratinga auricapilla*) resembles the Sun and the Jandaya but has considerably more green plumage. The forehead and crown are gold and red, the breast and rump are red, and the remainder of the bird is green. The length is about twelve inches.

The Peach-Fronted Conure (*Aratinga aurea*) is mostly green,

Facing page, top: Sun Conure, *Aratinga solstitialis,* adult male. He has produced over a dozen chicks in less than a year. *Bottom:* Jandaya Conure, *Aratinga jandaya,* nine weeks old.

Above: Juvenile Jandaya taking apple from a "Nansun." Both were hand-reared and have been kept as our own pets. The Jandaya loves to be handled, while "Spot" is something of a talker.

Peach-fronted Conure, *Aratinga aurea*, 12 weeks old. Such hand-reared youngsters make excellent pets and can be taught to talk.

Orange-fronted Conure, *Aratinga canicularis*, adult male. This species is one of our long-time favorite pets.

Dusky-headed Conure, *Aratinga weddellii*, 3 months old. Its beak has not yet turned completely black. A hand-reared Dusky is one of the sweetest pets.

with the forehead and feathers surrounding the eyes having an orange color. There is some blue on the crown bordering the orange of the forehead, and there is blue on the wing feathers. The beak is black. Immature birds often have less orange on the forehead and around the eyes. The length of the bird is about ten and one-half inches. This species is not as noisy as some of the other conures. Their voices are somewhat hoarse-sounding, but not high pitched. They are usually good breeders.

The Orange-fronted Conure (*Aratinga canicularis*) resembles the Peach-fronted Conure and is often confused with it. The most obvious difference is that the upper mandible of the Orange-fronted is a horn color, not dark. Also, this species has a bare eye ring. The mostly green plumage is set off by the orange of the forehead and some blue on the crown. Immature birds have dark eyes and less orange on the head. The length is about nine and one-half inches.

On the Cactus Conure (*Aratinga cactorum*) the

forehead and upper breast are pale brown, with a little blue on the crown. The back of the head, back, and wings are green, with the abdomen a yellow-orange color. The beak and feet are grayish. Immatures are duller in color, the crown being bluish and the abdomen olive with little orange to it. The length is ten inches. Cactuses are somewhat quieter than some of the other conures. Their voice is similar to that of the Peach-fronted Conure.

The Dusky-headed Conure (*Aratinga weddellii*) is mostly green with a grayish brown head. The wings and tail are blue and green. The beak and feet are blackish. Immatures are similar to parents but with dark eyes. The length is about eleven inches.

The Mitred Conure (*Aratinga mitrata*) is a very large and heavy-looking bird of about fifteen inches. The forehead, lores, and part of the cheeks are red. There are scattered red feathers on the throat, thighs, and elsewhere in the plumage. The overall coloring of the bird is green. The beak is a horn color.

On the Red-masked Conure (*Aratinga erythrogenys*) the plumage is again mostly green. Compared with the Mitred, the red is more extensive, from the crown, behind the eyes, and onto the cheeks. More red appears on the bend of the wings, and the thighs are also red. The beak is a horn color, and the iris is yellow. It measures about thirteen inches in length.

The Blue-crowned Conure (*Aratinga acuticaudata*) is a bird with mostly green plumage and the head a dull blue color. Some birds have their breasts lightly washed in blue. The upper

Cactus Conure *Aratinga cactorum cactorum*, the male of our breeding pair.

Blue-crowned Conure, *Aratinga acuticaudata*. This hen and her mate qualify as excellent parents. While they were raising three young of their own, they also fed three Yellow-collared Macaw chicks.

Red-masked Conure, *Aratinga erythrogenys*. In less than a year this male and his mate have produced clutches of three eggs six times. Most chicks were taken for hand-rearing, but the pair has had the opportunity to completely raise three chicks—successfully.

mandible is horn colored with a gray tip, and the lower part is blackish in some subspecies. The iris is orange, and the bare skin surrounding the eye is white. Immatures have less blue. The length is about fifteen inches.

The Brown-throated Conure (*Aratinga pertinax*) is largely green, but the many subspecies are marked with varying hues of yellow, orange, and brown from forehead to abdomen. All have brown in the throat area, though, and the dark beak keeps this species from being confused with others. The length

Brown-throated Conure *Aratinga pertinax pertinax*, adult male. One of the most brightly colored of the fourteen *pertinax* subspecies, this form is quite rare in captivity.

Nanday Conure, *Nandayus nenday*, adult hen. No one fails to mention that Nandays are very loud. But they are also excellent breeders, and hand-reared babies make very nice pets. If kept singly, they are not very loud, and they will learn to talk.

is eleven inches.

The Nanday Conure (*Nandayus nenday*) is closely related to the aratingas. It is a very popular bird, quite attractively colored. The basic color is bright green, with the beak and head black. The flight feathers are a bluish green. The feet are black, and the feathers on the thighs are bright red. The length is about twelve inches. Nandays are very good breeders. The only problem with them is that they can be very loud.

It is unfortunate that most of

the *Pyrrhura* species are rare in captivity. All but one species are native to South America. Many of the *Pyrrhura* conures are very similar to one another. They are close in size, ranging from eight and a half to twelve inches in length. Basically dark green, most have scalloped markings on the throat, neck, and upper breast.

Pyrrhuras are much quieter than aratingas. Though we own many different pairs, we never hear them; you would not even know that most of them were there. This makes them excellent

Green-cheeked Conure *Pyrrhura molinae restricta* (*erect*) and Maroon-bellied Conure *Pyrrhura frontalis chiripepe,* both adult males. The differences in coloration apparent in a photograph are hard to capture in words. The blue in the plumage of the Green-cheek is a character of the subspecies *restricta.*

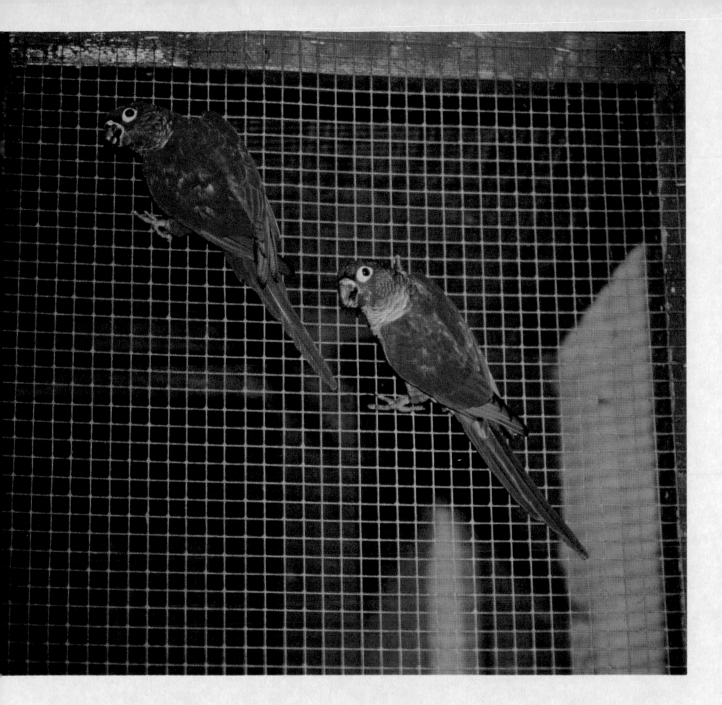

Maroon-bellied Conure *Pyrrhura frontalis chiripepe* (*above*), Green-cheeked Conure *Pyrrhura molinae restricta* (*below*). Another view of the same birds shown on the facing page. In the case of this Maroon-belly, the uniform color of the upper side of the tail indicates the subspecies *chiripepe*.

for apartments. They are not as destructive of wood, nor do they chew on wire mesh like some of the other conures. Ours seem to spend much of their time in the nest box. They go to nest easily and have good-sized clutches, usually four to six large eggs. Ours have always been excellent parents. In this genus, immature birds look very much like adults, in most cases. Hand-reared young *Pyrrhura* conures make remarkably good pets. The following are the three species most frequently available: The Maroon-bellied Conure

(*Pyrrhura frontalis*) is mostly dark green in color with a barred breast. There is some blue in the flight feathers, the tail is green with a dull reddish color at the tip and on the underside. There is a dull red on the abdomen. The eye ring is white, and the beak and legs are blackish. The length is about ten inches.

The Green-cheeked Conure (*Pyrrhura molinae*) looks much like the Maroon-bellied. They can be told apart by the brighter green cheeks and darker, brownish shade on the crown. Also, most of the

Left: Maroon-bellied Conure *Pyrrhura frontalis chiripepe*, adult male. We have found this subspecies to be very prolific, laying from four to eight eggs. With three clutches a year, we usually have more than fifteen chicks from our pair.

Facing page: Painted Conure, *Pyrrhura picta*, adult male.

Left: Green-cheeked Conure *Pyrrhura molinae restricta*, adult male.

Facing page: Brown-throated Conure *Aratinga pertinax chrysophrys*, adult male.

upper side of the tail of the Green-cheeks carries a maroon color.

The Painted Conure (*Pyrrhura picta*) is one of the most beautiful of the genus. This bird is brightly scalloped with white on the throat, neck, and upper breast and has white ear patches. The crown and nape are brown. Blue appears on the forecrown, cheeks, and at the base of the neck. There is red on the bend of the wings and maroon on the lores, upper cheeks, lower back, and abdomen. The rest of the body plumage is green. Some subspecies have some red on the head. The beak and legs are blackish. The length is nine inches.

Of the conures from other genera, two are common in aviculture. The Slender-billed Conure (*Enicognathus leptorhynchus*) has a very long, narrow upper mandible. Overall, the feathers are green, darkly edged, but they are a dull reddish color on the forehead, abdomen, and tail. The Patagonian Conure (*Cyanoliseus patagonus*), eighteen inches in length, is olive-brown, with a broken white necklace, a bright yellow-and-red abdomen, and a blackish beak.

Hybrids   When two different species of conures breed and produce young, *hybrid* conures are the result. Hybrid conures may or may not be sterile. The more closely related the parent species are (members of the same genus, for example), the more likely it is that their offspring will be fertile. If hybrids are produced, it is best that they go for pets and are not used for breeding. If hybrids are mated with pure birds repeatedly, the result could be birds that would

Slender-billed Conure, *Enicognathus leptorhynchus*, adult male. Slender-bills are real clowns, always playing and hanging from the wire. If there is a dirt floor, they love to dig. They also love to tip over their food and water crocks.

Green Conure, *Aratinga holochlora*, adult hen. This is the nominate subspecies, *holochlora holochlora*.

Patagonian Conure,
Cyanoliseus patagonus,
adult male. Also called
Burrowing Parrots
because of their nesting
behavior in the wild,
captive Patagonians are
usually hearty chewers of
perches and nest boxes.

look pure but in fact are not.
This means that if an unusual
color would appear in the
offspring of a pair of birds you
think are pure, it would be hard
to determine whether this is the
result of hybridization in the past
or is a real mutation.

The most commonly crossed
conures are the Jandaya Conure
and the Sun Conure; their
offspring are called "Sunday"
Conures. The main reason these
are crossed so frequently is
because there are many more
male Jandaya Conures than
hens and more hen Sun

Conures than males. The offspring resemble the Jandaya Conure, with the red and gold brighter in color. Some of these hybrids have some gold flecking on their shoulders and backs, which comes from the Sun Conure.

You will find that there are many species of conures in which it is difficult to obtain one sex or the other. Another example is the Golden-capped Conure, for which there are far more males than females. I have produced several babies by crossing a male Golden-capped Conure with a female Nanday Conure. I had the male Golden-capped in a breeding cage all by himself. He sat in the cage for months without a mate. When I acquired a Nanday hen, I put her in the cage with him for company. Two weeks later the Nanday hen was discovered to be on eggs. The offspring have a blackish brown on the top of the head and down to the eyes. There are red feathers surrounding the eyes, and the sides of the face by the beak. The abdomen is very orange, as are the undersides of the wings. The flight and tail feathers are blue, with the basic body color of the bird being green. Some of these hybrids have red socks, while others have brown—they all vary in coloring. Some have a very bright red-orange abdomen and also red-orange under the wings. All these hybrids, which we call the "Nancapped" Conure, have turned out to be tame and beautiful pets. The oldest one is talking and has learned many tricks.

Another hybrid that I have bred is the "Nansun" Conure, which is the result of a male Nanday Conure and a female Sun Conure (again because the male Sun Conures are not easily obtainable). Their offspring very much resembles the "Nancapped" Conure, except that there is more red on the face. Some have orange socks and orange on the back. The basic color of these birds is green, with the chest feathers being a lighter shade of green. Both the "Nancapped" and the "Nansun" conures have acquired the slightly larger size of the Nanday Conure.

Many species of conures have been crossed. Some of the *Aratinga* conures have mated with *Pyrrhura* conures and produced young.

Nevertheless, it is always best to pair birds of the same species whenever possible. The only time I allow hybridization is when I have conures of different species and each has no mate. I sometimes put the two birds together for company while my husband and I continue to search for appropriate mates. Once we obtain a mate for one or both of the birds, the pair is split up.

Determining Sex It is very difficult to tell the sex of conures. In every species, differences in appearance between the sexes are too slight or variable to be relied on.

Some people believe that the males have a larger head and a seemingly broader beak than the females. Individual birds vary quite a bit in size, so it is very difficult to pick out a pair by the size of the beak or head. I have not found that this method works for me.

Another way to try to determine if you have a pair is to observe them. If you have many conures in a flight, it is possible to watch them and separate the birds that have developed a pair bond (preening and feeding each other and

Facing page: Hispaniolan x Nanday, which might as well be called "Spanday" Conures. These 3-month-old youngsters were a gift from their breeder, Tony Silva. Surgical sexing has proved both to be hens. So far, they seem to be even louder than Nandays.

Facing page: The Nanday Conure is 3 months old, while the "Nansun"—Spot —is 6 months old. Spot got her name because for a while she had only a single small spot of red feathers. We've noticed that, like her Sun Conure parent, it will take her more than a year to become fully colored.

30

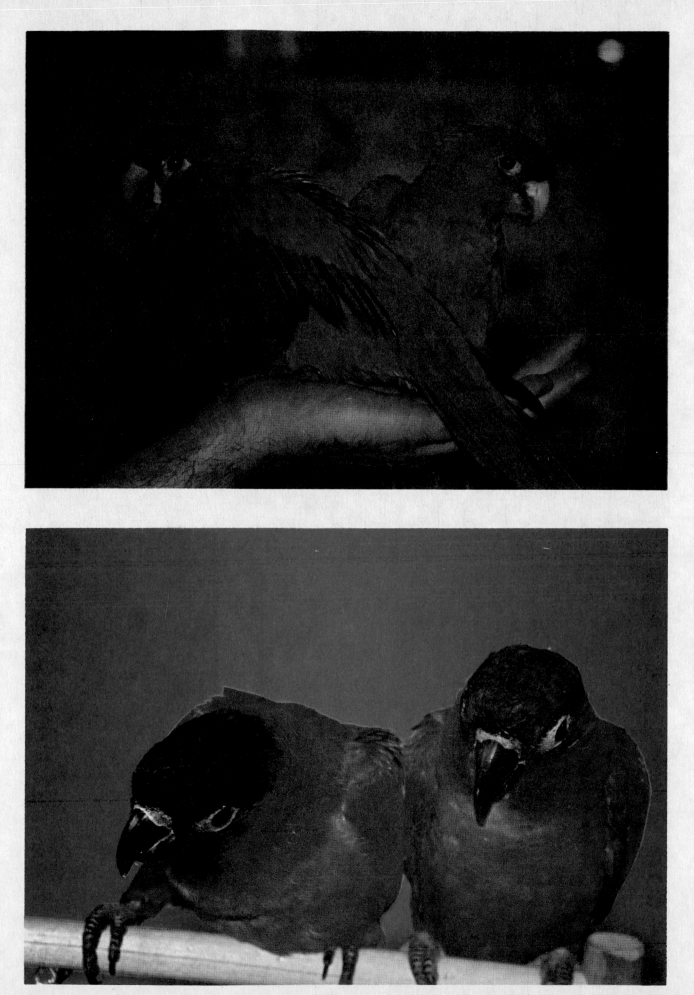

A young "Nancapped" Conure, the offspring of a Golden-capped father and a Nanday mother. As this 11-week-old chick matures, more red-orange will appear on the face and abdomen. Since both the Gold-cap and the Nanday are fully colored in about a year's time, the same can be expected of their progeny.

A male Brown-throat (*A. p. chrysophrys*) and a Peach-fronted hen hatched and raised a single chick, shown here at 3 months of age.

These 12-week-old hand-reared chicks are "Nansuns." The one looking at the camera is Spot.

always staying together). Remember, the only way to determine true pairs with this method is to have at least six birds together in a flight. If you put just two birds together in a cage to observe them, they will sometimes develop a pair bond; but this does not always mean that they are a true pair (male and female). For example, I have had two true male conures feed and preen each other and act as if they were just about ready to go to nest.

We determine the sex of our birds by surgical sexing. We have our vet, Dr. Max E. Weiss, do this for us. It is a very simple procedure, and the birds are just fine soon afterwards, as if nothing had happened. A small incision is made on one side of the bird near the rib cage. An endoscope or laparoscope is inserted into the opening. The vet can tell what sex the bird is,

whether it is old enough to breed, and sometimes its approximate age. Also, with this procedure the vet can tell if the bird is in good health and in breeding condition at present.

When we go to purchase conures and there are many to select from, we pick them out first by the pelvic-bone method. There are two small bones just in front of the vent area. Females have pelvic bones set far apart so the eggs can pass between them. Males, on the other hand, have their pelvic bones very close together, and usually the bones feel somewhat sharper. The only big problem is that immature conures do not have their pelvic bones set, so you can easily make a wrong choice. Also, there is an exception to every rule, and with some birds, the pelvic-bone method just will not work.

My husband is the one who

picks out our birds, and he has been ninety-percent right using the pelvic-bone method. He checks numerous birds pelvically until we feel we have selected what we need. Then, to determine each bird's sex and to find out the state of its health, we have them surgically sexed. I will say one thing: if we did not use both methods for sexing, we would be purchasing many birds of the same sex. We have found that the pelvic-bone method followed by surgical sexing is very successful for putting together true pairs.

Having a Vet Nowadays, with birds becoming very popular as pets and with many people breeding them, more and more vets are starting to specialize in the treatment of birds. If you do not have a vet who is experienced in treating birds, there are various ways to find one. You can contact your local pet shop and ask them to recommend one, or you can contact local bird breeders or bird clubs. Often a vet who does not specialize in birds will recommend one who does.

It is sometimes possible to treat a bird yourself if a problem arises, but there are situations where a good bird vet is a necessity. It is very important to be able to contact a good veterinarian at any time, in case an emergency should occur. A vet knows the correct medication and dosage for a particular illness. Many bird diseases cannot be diagnosed without lab tests. If you run into any questionable problems, it is best if you call your vet immediately. Sometimes this can save a bird's life.

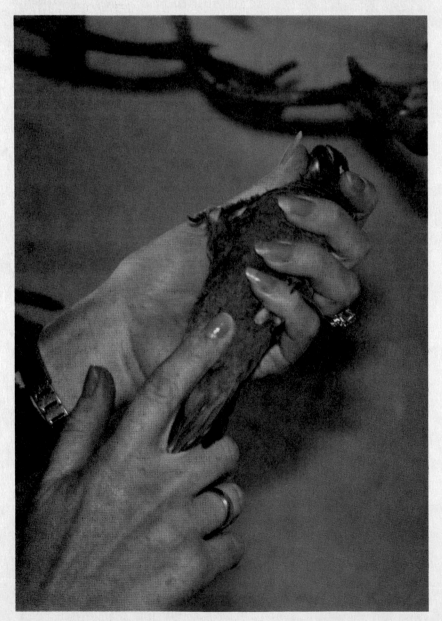

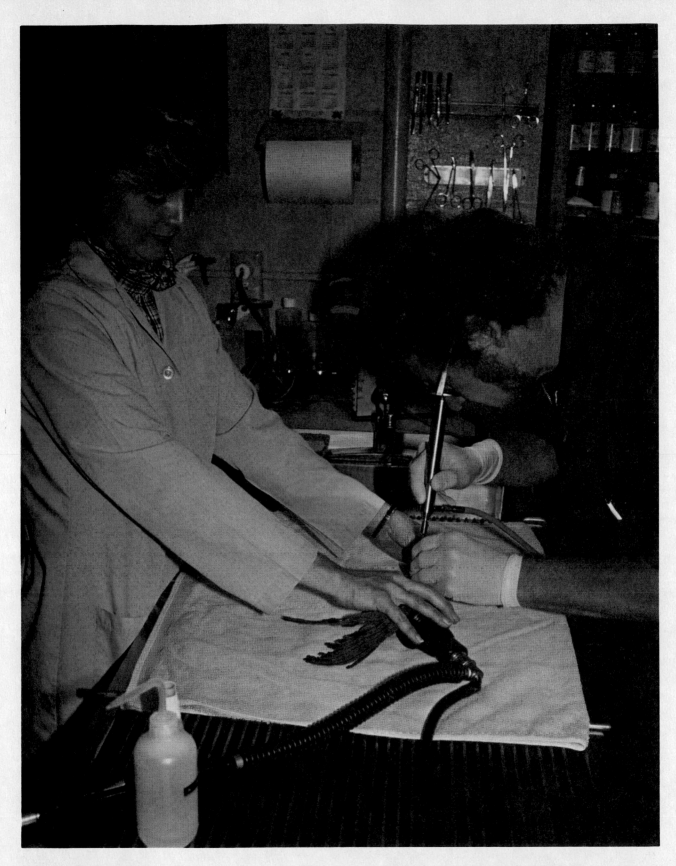

Facing page, top: White-eyed Conure undergoing anesthesia, prior to surgical sexing. *Bottom:* Checking the pelvic bones of a Maroon-bellied Conure.

Above: Seeing the testes or ovaries through the laparoscope, Dr. Weiss can tell whether the White-eye is mature enough to breed. Other organs can also be inspected, to assess their health.

Dusky-headed Conures, *Aratinga weddellii*, 3 months old.

Housing Conures

Quarantining New Birds It is very important to quarantine all new birds before they are added to your existing stock, even if they have just come out of a quarantine station. This is done as a precaution, just in case the new birds are harboring or coming down with an illness. If the new birds are carrying a disease and are housed together with the stock you already own, it could be disastrous. It's unfortunate that some diseases cannot be detected until it is too late. At least we can isolate all new, incoming birds for thirty days and hope for the best. Some people quarantine new birds in the same cage with healthy budgies or in another cage right next to them. Then, if any of the birds die, an autopsy is performed right away by the state lab or a vet to discover the cause of death.

Any new birds should be housed in an area where no other birds are being kept. It would be ideal, if possible, to quarantine the new birds at a friend's or a relative's house where there are no other birds. To prevent any illness from spreading, new birds should be tended to (fed, watered, cage cleaned, and so forth) last, after all your other birds have been taken care of for the day. Make sure you wash your hands very well after tending the new birds.

I observe the new birds very closely to make sure everything looks fine. If any of the birds look or act abnormally, I have our vet check the bird. Since most of our new birds are surgically sexed right after we get them, their health is also checked by our vet at this time. This way, we have an idea right from the start whether the new birds are healthy.

If we know the background of the new birds—that they were home-bred by breeders who are very conscientious—we quarantine them for twenty to thirty days. If the new birds came from a commercial quarantine station, pet shop, or a private party via a newspaper ad, we quarantine them for a full thirty days. It's really best to isolate all new birds for the full thirty days. Since there are many bird diseases being spread around now, quarantining every new bird is the best protection.

Acclimating A bird that has been kept indoors must be acclimated to weather outdoors. In the cool months, this should be done slowly. If the weather is 55 F. or more, the bird can be put outside for the day and taken indoors for the night. You

should follow this procedure for about one month before leaving the bird outside for the night. I have found that the warm summer months are the best time of the year to acclimate conures. When the weather is warm and the temperature does not drop below 55 F. at night, a conure can be left permanently outdoors at once. Most conures sleep in their nest boxes all night. Because of this habit, I've found, conures are fairly easy to acclimate to the outdoor weather that we have. Just be sure that you keep a very close watch on birds when acclimating them. You must take them back indoors at the first sign of any possible illness (fluffed feathers or not bright-eyed). If you purchase conures from someone who has kept them outdoors in weather similar to what you have, the birds can be put directly in an aviary or cage

outdoors, as they are already acclimated.

Worming   When birds are kept outdoors, there are many kinds of worms they can get, but it seems like roundworms are the most common. If a bird has worms and is left untreated for too long, it can die. If you suspect that you may have a problem, your vet can run a quick lab test to see exactly what kind of worms you may be dealing with. Then the birds can be treated for that particular type of worm.

   I use Tramisol in powder form for worming my birds; it is good for almost all types of worms that birds may have. I have used it on all my birds, with very good results. I mix one teaspoon of the powdered form into three gallons of drinking water. This can be left before the birds for two days in cool weather. If the

Above: Aviaries in our back yard. The plants in front of the aviaries give the birds privacy and shade from the hot summer sun.

Facing page, top: Twice a month the floors of all the aviaries are raked clean of droppings and seed hulls. *Below:* My daughter Debra likes to supervise while I'm cleaning. The flight beside her has over thirty conure breeding cages inside.

38

weather is quite warm, I leave it for only a day and a half. Then the birds are put back on fresh drinking water.

As a precaution, I worm my birds twice a year. If you find that the birds definitely have worms, then they should receive the above treatment twice, with two weeks in between.

I once had a lovebird which one day could not fly. I took the bird inside the house and examined it. The bird seemed to be in fairly good health; her cere was clean, her droppings looked normal, and she had a good appetite. The only thing was that she was somewhat on the thin side, and she could not fly. I decided to put some Tramisol in her drinking water. In a few hours, she had passed innumerable worms; they were thin and about a half-inch long: roundworms. The next day she was much stronger, and within a few days she was flying again.

Just remember, it is best if you check with your vet before using Tramisol or any other worming medication on your birds.

Cages and Aviaries Conures can be bred successfully in cages or aviaries, indoors or out. Which set-up you choose will depend on personal preference, as well as on the amount of space you have available.

You can purchase aviaries and cages, or you can construct your own. It's not difficult to build an aviary or a cage; any handy person can do it. My husband and I built all our aviaries out of wood and wire in our spare time. We have over thirty outdoor flights around our home near Los Angeles. Many are six feet high, three feet wide, and eight feet deep. Others are six by eight in area and eight feet high. A few are even larger.

There is no particular reason why some aviaries are six feet high and others eight feet. All we have done is to make use of all the space we have. Some aviaries may have been built taller or wider so we could cage-breed inside the flights.

As is usual, each of our flights has one pair of birds inside, set up for breeding. In addition, however, each flight may contain, say, three cages, all of which house pairs of conures. For example, one flight 3 x 8 x 6 feet high may have a pair of Cockatiels set up inside. But besides being a breeding space for the Cockatiels, the flight also serves as a safety enclosure for the three pairs of conures kept in cages.

I have found that it makes no difference which species of conures are housed in the flight. What I prefer is to have three different species in the cages (Suns, Jandayas, and Nandays, for example). Thus, if two birds should escape from their cages into the flight at the same time, there is no guessing about which should go back where. The escapees can be returned to the right cages immediately.

It is important, though, that in any enclosure, whether cage or flight, only one pair of conures is set up for breeding. This way, there is no fighting over nest boxes or mates.

If you decide to aviary-breed your conures, it doesn't matter what size the flight is. The most important thing is that it will hold the conures securely. Conures love to chew on wood when they have free time (which can be most of the day). If your aviary is constructed of wood, it is very important that all the wood be covered with sheet metal or wire mesh. I have heard many stories of conures

In these flights the cockatiels are free, while conures are kept in the breeding cages.

40

A stack of four cages for
smaller conures: Duskies,
Peach-fronts, and Cactus,
for example.

chewing right through 2x4s in a
couple of days and escaping
from the newly built aviary. If
the flights we build are to house
conures, all wood is covered
with 1/4-inch-square wire mesh.

For the sides and roofs of our
flights, we have successfully
used three sizes of welded wire:
1 x 1/2 inch, 1/2 inch square, and
1/4 x 1/2 inch. The last will help
prevent rodents from entering
and eating up your profits (food,
eggs, and sometimes even
birds); it is the size mesh we
now try to use when
constructing cages.

Also, whatever size mesh the
wire is, make sure that it is fairly
heavy gauge. I had a pair of
conures that chewed a large
round hole right through 1/2-inch
wire. Fortunately, the hole
opened into the neighboring
flight, so the birds weren't able
to escape.

Some of our aviaries are
simply built on bare ground and
have dirt floors. Others have
cement or wire bottoms, to keep
out mice.

The back part of each flight
(the area away from the door) is
covered. About three feet of the
roof has plywood topped with
fiberglass, so the birds can get
out of the rain. This is where the
conure breeding cages are
located. We don't use heaters in
any of the aviaries; all our birds
are acclimated to the weather,
which at times can get as cold as
28 F.

Some winters we staple plastic
sheeting on the more exposed
sides, to keep out rain on very
windy days. The main reason
for this is so that the feed does
not get damp and become
moldy. When we have a mild
winter, no plastic is needed, and
the birds do just fine.

Along the fronts of the flights
we have a variety of plants
growing. They help shade the

41

flights and cages from the hot sun in the summer months and also shield the birds from the wind. There are no plants inside the flights.

Our aviaries are painted and look nice, but they are not that fancy. They do look neat, as the wood is painted green. The wire is black so you can see the birds inside better.

So far as cages are concerned, the size of a cage should be determined by the size of the conures you intend to house in it. I have bred Maroon-bellied and Cactus conures in cages 16 x 16 x 48 inches long, with a standard Cockatiel nest box attached to the outside of the cage. Some of my cages are small (an 18-inch cube for Duskies) and some quite large (3 x 3 x 6 feet long), depending on the conures I want to keep in them.

All cages are located in flights or larger safety cages, so if any bird escapes from its cage, it will not get away. I have had conures open their cage doors, even with hooks and latches securing them. Some conures will chew a hole in their nest box and gain their freedom that way. These are the times when safety measures are crucial. Just one escape, and that little extra precaution pays for itself.

With cage breeding it is very easy to keep your birds healthy and clean by having a wire bottom on the cage. This way, all extra fruit and vegetables fall through and do not become spoiled while still within the birds' reach. The droppings also fall through the bottom, which keeps the birds clean.

Though we do not breed any of our conures indoors, they can be bred in your living quarters,

Plastic sheeting against the winter weather has been installed on this conure-breeding flight.

42

Fred is helping serve the soft-food mix. The wire boxes hold soft-food dishes and water crocks for the cages into which they open. Six feet long by three feet square, these are used for breeding larger parrots and conures, such as Slender-bills, Mitreds, and African Greys.

basement, attic, or garage. Just be sure that where the birds are housed does not get too hot in the summer. Our birds can take the 100 F. summer heat outdoors, but in a poorly ventilated attic or garage, it can become very stuffy. In these situations a fan or a cooler can be helpful, but don't let the breeze blow directly on the birds, lest they become ill.

I have seen some indoor set-ups where various-sized cages (similar to ours) were used for breeding. The owners were doing just fine, raising many chicks. If there were no windows for light, artificial light was used. Some breeders had fluorescents, while others used standard light bulbs. In most cases, the lights were on for at least fourteen hours.

Perches Perches used for conures should range from ¾ to 1½ inches in diameter, depending on the size of the conures. For example, an Orange-fronted should have a perch about ¾ inch, while perches for the large Patagonian Conure should be about 1½ inches in diameter. If the perches are not suited to the size of the bird, foot problems may occur.

Perches can be cleaned by rubbing them with sandpaper. Clean off the dust before replacing the perches in the cage, so the birds do not inhale the dirt and dust. If you wash the perches, do not put them back until they are dry, or the birds might catch cold.

Dowels or tree branches can be used, as they can easily be replaced. The birds seem to enjoy natural branches, since grasping them appears to be easier. They also like to chew on the branches, which is good for their beaks. Fruit-tree branches

are ideal. Just be sure that the
branches have not been sprayed
with any insect poison! Also
make sure that the perches are
not loose, or mating may be
incomplete, resulting in infertile
eggs.

Nest Boxes The size of the
nest box also depends on the
size of the conures which will be
going to use it. Most of our
conures seem to like the
standard Cockatiel nest box,
which measures about twelve
inches square and fourteen
inches tall. Some of the very
large conures should have a nest
box a little larger because of
their enormous size (such as the
Patagonian Conure).

Once in a while I come across
a pair of conures that insist on
emptying all their nesting
material out of the nest box.
Without some nesting material in
the box, the birds may crack

their eggs on the hard wooden
base of the nest box when
jumping in the box, or the eggs
may be damaged by rolling
around on the bare bottom.
What I do with such pairs is to
give them a nest box which is
twelve inches square but about
twenty-four inches tall. Wire
mesh is attached inside the box
from the entrance hole all the
way down to the bottom so they
can use it as a ladder. This helps
the birds to climb in and out, so
they will not jump on their eggs.
With about six inches of
shavings in such a deep nest
box, the birds cannot possibly
empty out all of it.

All the nest boxes I use are
made of wood. Conures usually
do chew on their nest boxes,
which seems to be a natural part
of their nesting behavior; but
once they are ready to go to
nest, most pairs stop. It is very
important to keep a careful

Conure carpenters have
their own ideas about how
a nest box should be
remodeled. These are
standard Cockatiel
nest boxes.

44

The amount of pine shavings I put in depends on the depth of the nest box.

watch on the nest box because once in a while a pair will chew their way right through the nest box. I had a pair of Nanday Conures that chewed a hole on the side of their nest box that did not face me. Their cage was set up in a Cockatiel aviary, and when they got out, they killed a brood of baby Cockatiels. So please keep an eye on the box, and if they start a hole, replace the box. Another pair of conures, I'm told, were already sitting on eggs when they chewed a hole right through the bottom of their box. All the eggs fell out and broke. If a pair of conures already on eggs chew a hole in their box, I tack on a piece of heavy welded wire to cover the hole. If the box is changed while the conures are on eggs, they may not return to eggs placed in a new box.

Some people cover and line the nest box with sheet metal or wire—either will work. I prefer not to, but I exercise close surveillance.

The entrance hole of the nest box should be three to four inches in diameter, depending on the size of the conures. If the birds want a larger entrance hole, they will usually do their own remodeling. An outside perch or platform should be about two inches below the entrance hole so the pair can easily get in or out.

Most of our nest boxes have a hinged lid, so the top can be lifted up for inspection. Very tall boxes can have an inspection door on the side of the box about eight inches from the bottom. This door can be opened or slid to one side to inspect the nest at the level of the nesting material.

The nesting materials I use in our nest boxes are pine shavings and peat moss. I pour about half a cup of water in the bottom of the box, add a thin layer of damp peat moss, and finally put in a layer of pine shavings three to six inches deep, depending on the depth of the nest box. The water will keep the bottom of the nest box slightly damp, so the eggs will not become too dry. I clean out the nest box thoroughly after each brood, when the babies have left. The box is sprayed with a good mite spray, aired out in the sun for two days, and then reinstalled. The mite spray used must be made especially for use around birds without harming them.

If the nest box is too big, problems can arise. Eggs can get lost in the box if the pair knocks them away from the clutch. Also, if the box is too large, in very cold weather the chicks can more easily chill and die when the parents go out of the nest box to eat and drink. Sometimes a baby will crawl into a corner and go unnoticed; it will soon become chilled and die. At times, conures given a choice between a Cockatiel and a budgie nest box will choose the budgie box to nest in. You can experiment with different-sized nest boxes with pairs of birds that have not wanted to go to nest.

If a pair of conures are set up for breeding in a flight, I put in at least two nest boxes in different locations; also the boxes will be of different sizes. For example, one will be a Cockatiel nest box, while the other will be somewhat larger or smaller, depending on the size of the conures.

Though I had owned one particular pair of Dusky-headed Conures for over a year, they just would not show any interest in going to nest. I decided to change their nest box, which at that time was a standard

In this flight a tall nest box has been attached to the outside of a cage containing Jandaya Conures. This pair insist on throwing all the pine shavings out of the shorter nest boxes. With the 24-inch box, there is still a thick layer left when the hen lays.

A Golden-capped pair were set up temporarily in a flight until their breeding cage was ready. Many people choose to breed their conures in a set-up like this. The male is in the foreground.

Cockatiel box, for an English-budgie nest box. The Duskies were thrilled with their new box; two weeks after the change the pair went to nest, laid two fertile eggs, and raised both chicks.

If you are cage breeding, the nest box should be securely attached to the outside of the cage. A hole large enough for the birds should be cut through the cage mesh where the nest box entrance hole will be. The nest box should be made removable so it can be cleaned out after the babies have left the nest.

Conures use their nest box for roosting as well as for nesting. Almost all my conures sleep in their nest boxes at night. Also, many of them rush into the box when they get scared. The nest box is their hideaway and is kept in place for them all year around.

Carrying Cages It's advisable to have carrying cages on hand. These are wooden boxes with the top covered with wire mesh or with mesh windows on the sides. The wire is there so the bird has ventilation and so it can

be observed. Carrying cages of various sizes can be bought, or they can be home-made. Some cages have a divider to make two cages of one, for easy carrying. This allows each member of a pair to be transported in its own separate compartment so no fighting can occur. There should be only one door for each compartment, which should close securely so there is no chance of escape. There should also be a handle on the top of the cage for carrying convenience. These cages are very handy for traveling with a conure.

If you are going a short distance, it will not be necessary to put water into the carrying cage. Usually the water just spills, and the bird ends up wet. Seed, moist bread, and apple are all that's needed.

Make sure the cage is not in direct sunlight while traveling in a car. The heat from the sun can dehydrate the bird and kill it. Also, never leave a bird in a hot car with the windows up— this too will surely do a conure in. It is best to cover the carrying cage with a towel, as this helps keep the bird as calm and quiet as possible. If the conure gets excited and starts to jump around in the cage, it could injure itself. Try not to startle the bird. If the weather is very hot, the towel can be dampened, which will help to keep the bird cool.

You will find that carrying cages are quite useful. I always have one in the car, for I never know when I'm going to come home with a new conure or two.

Useful Accessories There are a few other items you'll probably need if you keep conures.

A bird net is vitally important.

A Nanday and a Red-mask atop a carrying cage suitable for transporting two conures.

48

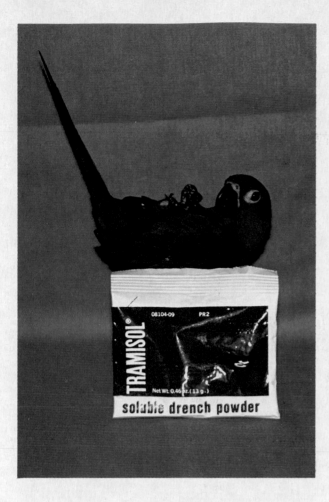

Left: "Tramisol" is a trade name for levamisole, which is currently the most widely used treatment for roundworms. The model is "Sunny," our pet Jandaya Cónure. *Right:* Sun Conure at 7 weeks old, the age of fledging.

Without a net, it is not easy to catch a conure in full flight in an aviary. Nets come in many sizes. The diameter should be at least ten inches. The length of the handle depends on where the net is going to be used. If the net is for taking a conure out of a cage, the handle should be about twelve inches long; but if you are going to use it in a large aviary, the handle should be much longer. Nylon bird nets can be purchased at most pet shops.

Gloves are sometimes needed for handling conures, so you will not be bitten. Leather gloves, in which you can move your fingers easily, are the best. I also use a towel for handling birds. The bird can easily be wrapped in it to be checked over or just transferred to another cage.

Some of the accessories I have for my birds are nail clippers for trimming nails and beaks, small holding cages, extra feed cups, extra nest boxes, styptic powder to stop bleeding (baby or bath powder can also be used, in case of an emergency) and various medications. As time goes on, you too will build up a supply of accessories for your birds.

Cactus Conures *Aratinga cactorum cactorum*, adult pair.

Feeding Conures

Feeders Various kinds of feeders that can be purchased will work successfully with your birds. There are also several ways to feed your birds.

The feeders with partitions and a glass front are particularly nice. With the glass front you can see when the birds are running low on seed, at just a glance. Some of these feeders have three compartments, so sunflower, safflower, and budgie mix can be put in separately. This allows the birds to eat the seed they want without kicking out all the rest, looking for the favorite ones. Also, most of these feeders will hold a supply of seed sufficient for a pair of birds for about five days.

Feeders should be made of metal. With most conures the wooden feeders would not last too long. Remember, conures love to chew on wood.

Metal rabbit feeders of all sizes are available. Three of these feeders set up in each cage or aviary will do just fine, still permitting the birds to choose only the seeds they want to eat, without scattering the others.

Another way to feed conures is to use ceramic bowls (crocks). Crocks will fit your needs easily, as they come in all sizes. You can set them up with different kinds of seed in each one.

There are probably many more ways to feed your birds. Some pairs of birds cannot use a feeder that holds a large supply because they like to empty out all the seeds before they eat any. For these birds I suggest the crock method of feeding. As I have mentioned before, you will end up feeding your birds in the way that suits your needs and your birds best.

In our set-up, each aviary and cage also has a small bowl of health grit mixed with oyster shells, a mineral block, and a cuttlebone to round out the birds' diet. The grit with oyster shells helps the birds grind up their food and also has minerals which are needed to keep the birds in good health. The cuttlebone and mineral block provide calcium and salt and also help to keep the birds' beaks trim.

Dry Seed Many different kinds of foods should be fed if conures are to have a well-balanced diet. With proper care and nutrition you will have much healthier and prettier birds, that should go to nest and produce big and healthy babies.

Various seeds form a large part of a conure diet. Our conures have sunflower seed, safflower seed, and Budgerigar

mix always available. I feel that conures should have food before them at all times. The birds are fed cafeteria-style so they can choose what seeds they want to eat at any time. Also, by feeding each type of seed separately there will be less wasted food. This way, for example, when you go to change the food and find only sunflower seed was eaten that day, you will not have to throw away the other seeds that were not eaten.

I purchase all my seed for the conures in large 50- and 100-pound sacks. I buy enough seed to last all our birds one month. Purchasing the seed this way is quite a bit cheaper than buying it by the pound. Not everybody can buy so much at one time—this should be done only if you own a lot of birds. Remember, we have over two hundred birds. The seeds are transferred from their original

sacks to large metal trash cans. These are kept in a metal shed, where I store all my feed and supplies for the conures. Each kind of seed is put into a different trash can. With the lids on, the metal trash cans keep out insects, mice, and rats. Also, the seed stored in cans stays fresh, clean, and dry. Seed can be tested to see if it is fresh. If you are in doubt whether the seed is fresh, take about a handful and sprout it. At least ninety percent should sprout if the seed is fresh. Seed that is too old, dried out, and dead has no nutritive value for the birds.

Sprouted Seed   I have found that the birds enjoy sprouted seed, and as a result they seem to do much better when it comes to breeding. Sprouted seed is very nutritious for the birds and is easily digested by young chicks.

Safflower seed, budgerigar mix, gray-stripe sunflower seed, and monkey chow stored in metal trash cans, which are kept covered to keep moisture out. Handy scoops can be made by cutting the bottoms off plastic bottles.

Facing page: After soaking, seed put in a bucket with holes in the bottom will drain nicely. A heated knitting needle makes smooth-edged holes.

There are four kinds of seed that I sprout for my birds, but you can add additional ones if you wish. I will describe how I prepare my sprouted seed, but remember, you can ad-lib to your liking.

I use one cup each of sunflower and safflower seeds and one-quarter cup each of white millet and canary seed, mixing all four together in a plastic bucket. Next I add about one gallon of water with one teaspoon of calcium propionate, then mix the water and seeds together well. The calcium propionate is a preservative; it is very important that this be included to prevent the seed from molding. Calcium propionate can also prevent and cure crop mold, so in very small amounts it can be beneficial to the birds.

The seeds are left to soak in the bucket for eighteen to twenty-four hours. After they have soaked, they are then dumped into another bucket with many very small holes in the bottom. The holes must be smaller than the seeds so they cannot go through. It is best if the entire bottom of the bucket is perforated, like a colander.

The way I make holes in the bottom of a bucket is to use a thin rod (like a knitting needle) about twelve inches long. I heat the rod over an open flame. When the rod is very hot, I start to puncture holes in the bottom of the bucket until the rod must be heated up again. With this method, all the holes are melted smooth. You will find it much easier to stir the seeds if the holes are smooth. You can also use a drill to make holes on the bottom of the bucket, but you will find that the holes will be somewhat rough.

After the seeds are put into the bucket with the holes, they

should be rinsed well with cold water. The seeds remain in this bucket for twenty-four to forty-eight hours, until they start to sprout. In warmer weather the seeds sprout faster, but in cooler weather it takes a little longer. It is a good idea if you periodically stir the seeds to prevent them from sticking together and spoiling—stirring will keep the seeds loose and fresh. When they start to sprout, it is time to feed them to the birds. The sprouted seeds can also be stored in the refrigerator for two or three days. You must discard the entire bucket of sprouted seeds at any sign of mold or spoilage.

Fruits and Vegetables A large variety of fruits and vegetables can be fed to conures. Each day my conures receive apples, oranges, peas (fresh or frozen), corn (fresh or frozen), carrots that have been chopped or grated, grated beets, and chopped spinach. Once a week I include some other fruit or vegetable, to vary their diet. I might add grapes, pomegranate, romaine lettuce, plums, pears, banana, peaches, or dry dog kibble or monkey chow. I never feed my birds avocado at all! It has been known to kill birds. I know of many pet birds that were fed avocado and died within twenty-four hours after eating it. Some birds can not digest this fruit and will die if they eat it.

With my conures, I have found that you can control the breeding cycle by means of their diet. When fruit and vegetables are cut out of their diet, most of the conures will not nest. As soon as the normal diet is returned, most will go to nest

Many kinds of fruits and vegetables are good for conures—these are some of what we feed ours.

54

Sprouted seed and chopped fruits and vegetables, still in their refrigerator-storage containers, prior to being mixed.

and lay eggs within two weeks.

You may find a pair of conures that refuse to eat any fruits or vegetables. The only thing that you can do is to continue to offer them a large variety, until they find something they like. I have had conures that refused all fruits and vegetables, but I continued to offer them some every day. Some pairs have gone without touching any of this for as long as nine months; then, all of a sudden, they start to eat everything and go to nest. The main thing is that you should still offer them a large variety of foods, as you never know when they are going to decide to start to eat a varied diet.

Never use spoiled or rotten fruits or vegetables. Make sure all fruits and vegetables are washed thoroughly before feeding them to your birds, to be

sure they are free from insecticide. When feeding your birds, just remember to use common sense!

Preparing Soft Food Now I'll explain how I prepare a well-rounded diet for my conures. I cut up washed apples, oranges, and spinach, and put each separately in large sealed plastic containers, which are put in the refrigerator. With the fruits and vegetables cut into small pieces, the birds can easily hold the pieces in their feet and eat them. Also, I have found that if such food is cut into small pieces, most of what goes uneaten will dry up instead of turning rotten.

The reason I prefer to use spinach over other greens is that there is quite a lot of vitamins and iron in spinach, which is excellent for conures. Also, there is very little water in

55

Left: Soft-food mix: sprouted seed, fruits, and vegetables. *Right:* Some of the supplements used in my soft-food mix and hand-rearing diets.

spinach, so the conures will not get watery droppings from eating it. Lettuce can give the birds diarrhea. Beets are also high in vitamins, and the birds really seem to enjoy eating them: roots, stems, and leaves.

I next take about one pound each of frozen peas and corn kernels, put them together in a large bowl and add hot water so they will thaw. In the meantime I grate two large carrots. I then drain all the water from the peas and corn. When this has drained well, I mix in the grated carrots. I put this mixture (peas, corn, and carrots) in a large sealed plastic container and put it in the refrigerator. Last, I grate beets and put them in another plastic container, in the refrigerator. Now I have all my fruits and vegetables ready to use when I need them. In sealed containers in the refrigerator they will keep for two or three days, so I don't have to bother cutting up fruits and vegetables daily.

There are no exact proportions to the amounts of fruits and vegetables in my mix. Some days, for example, I may add more apple and on other days more corn. I add more of the kind of food that the birds seem to be eating most.

Every morning I take a large bowl and put in sprouted seeds (sunflower, safflower, millet, and canary). I add just a little cod-liver oil and wheat-germ oil to the sprouted seeds and mix everything together very well until the seeds are lightly coated. Cod-liver oil keeps the birds in good health and gives their feathers sheen. Wheat-germ oil aids the reproductive cycle, increasing the production of fertile eggs. I then add a small amount of a good vitamin powder for birds and mix it in the sprouted seeds. Next, I add some of the cut-up fruits and vegetables (apples, oranges, spinach, corn, peas, carrots, beets, and whatever else) and

Dishes of soft food ready to be taken out to the breeding cages.

again mix well—this way the vitamins get onto everything.

If conures are fed properly with fresh seeds, fruits, and vegetables, very little additional vitamins are required. Too much vitamin supplement added to their food could do the birds more harm than good. Liver ailments are a common side effect in birds receiving too much vitamin supplement. So remember, if the birds are on a well-balanced diet, too little vitamin supplement is better than too much.

I spoon my soft-food mixture into individual dishes for each of my pairs of birds. Each pair receives about three tablespoons of this mix. If the pair has chicks, they receive more. You do not have to feed the sprouted seeds and fruits and vegetables mixed together. I do this because I have to feed about two hundred birds every day, and it is easier for me to have fewer dishes.

As time goes on and you get to know your birds, you will develop your own method of feeding, one that fits your lifestyle as well as that of your birds.

I feed all my conures this same diet every day throughout the year, whether they are nesting or not. This keeps the conures in top condition, strong and healthy at all times. The only difference in feeding is when a pair has chicks: as I've mentioned, they receive more of the soft-food mix. Conures that receive a good supply of various fresh seeds daily and fruits and vegetables at least twice a week will still go to nest and raise young.

Water To keep water fresh, it should be changed daily. Many conures deposit their fruit, seeds, and various other materials in the water. If left too long, this will foul the water. Our conures receive their water

Left: Sunny enjoys lying on her back; in my hand she'll play with her feet. I've also found her lying on her back in her seed bowl, cracking sunflower seeds.

Facing page: Breeding cages housing Suns and Jandayas, showing the copper tubing used in our automatic watering system.

Left: Sunny taking a bath in her water bowl.

Facing page: Frequent bathing gives a beautiful shine to the feathers. The bird in the foreground is the male of this Sun Conure pair.

in ceramic bowls (crocks). This way, they use it for drinking and also for bathing. Most conures love to take a daily bath. This is especially important if the hen is on eggs, since keeping the eggs humid will make it easier for the chicks to hatch. Otherwise, the shells on the eggs could become too dry and hard for the chicks to break through. Another nice thing about using ceramic crocks is that they can easily be cleaned. They should be washed with a good disinfectant and detergent at least once a week. If you are lucky enough to own a dishwasher, they can be cleaned sufficiently in there.

My husband built a watering system for all our flights and cages. It works like an automatic sprinkler system. A timer turns it on every day for seven minutes, filling up the crocks and even cleaning them when the water overflows. Of course, the crocks still must be sponged out every few days. With this system, no bird is ever without water. The water comes directly from the tap.

Maroon-bellied Conures *Pyrrhura frontalis chiripepe*, 3 months old.

Breeding
Conures

What to Expect   Conures should have at least a full year to adjust to their surroundings before you start worrying whether they are going to breed. After a year of no results I start making some changes. I either change the nest box to a different-sized one, or I may even change the location of their cage. I add more fruits and vegetables to their diet. If another six months or so goes by with still no eggs, I may give each of the pair a different mate. Sometimes I have had conures that are just not compatible. Re-pairing these conures may bring about breeding results.

Speaking from my experiences with conures, I have found that some pairs of a given species require one kind of treatment, while other pairs of the same species have to be treated differently. For example, I have had many pairs of Jandaya Conures use Cockatiel nest boxes, whereas other Jandayas preferred very deep nest boxes. I cannot say that each species that I have bred should be treated in some specific way. Instead, you will have to discover the particular likes and dislikes of each pair of conures you own, no matter what species it is. Some will prefer to eat apple and others

corn; some will eat budgie mix, sunflower, and safflower seeds, while others eat only sunflower seeds and a little budgie mix. I have had some pairs of conures make a small "air hole" in the side of their nest box before laying their eggs. Some will go to nest in cages, while others prefer a large flight. By all means, I feel that each pair of conures should be treated as individuals, not according to what species they are. You should give them what is best for their needs.

Just what a pair needs may never become completely clear. Let me give you an example of what you may come up against. I had a proven male Jandaya that was once someone's pet. He had bred with a Sun Conure and produced "Sundays." I went and purchased another Jandaya that also had been a pet; when this one was surgically sexed, it turned out to be a hen. When the hen was put in with the male, he instantly attacked her, so I removed her (by the way, the cage was also new to the male). I tried again, and the same thing happened. The male was then removed for a while and later returned to the hen. He again attacked the hen, chasing and biting her. Fred and I were about ready to give up

when we decided to try one more thing. We took the two conures and put them into a cage right next to the one they had been fighting in. This time it was just like love at first sight. They started preening each other instantly, and he even started to feed her. Within five minutes the two were together in the nest box. Less than two weeks after they were put in the cage, she laid her first egg. To this day we have never been able to figure out why he would attack her in the other cage. Both cages were set up identically—in size, feeders, crocks, and nest box—and they were about six inches apart, side by side.

In captivity, many of our conures will breed almost all year around, with a rest during the hot summer months. As the weather starts to cool, our conures start to go back to nest, which is usually in the middle of the fall. They could rear four clutches a year, or even more, if

Above: A pair of Patagonian Conures. Of this pair, the male shows more red on the thighs.

Facing page, top: Our best breeding pair of Red-masks. In less than a year they have produced six clutches of three eggs each, which is very unusual for this species. *Bottom:* "Spanday" Conure, 3 months old.

the chicks are pulled for hand-rearing.

Occasionally, conures will go to nest when they are as young as nine months old. Usually males at such a young age are not mature enough to fertilize eggs. Sometimes hens at a very early age do not take proper care of their eggs. They may break the eggs, or they may not sit tightly and incubate the eggs properly. Or they may hatch out the babies but not feed them, or not brood them correctly. But once conures are about two years old, it seems that they do quite well. At this time they seem to settle down and get serious about raising young.

Courtship and Laying Eggs
Conures exhibit no specific courtship behavior, but they do develop a pair bond. A pair of conures will very often be seen feeding one another. Usually it is the male that feeds the hen, but if two conures are housed together and are the same sex, one may still feed the other. Conures will also preen each other whether they are a true pair or not. It seems that many conures prefer to mate (copulate) inside the nest box. Some do mate on the perch, but I have found that mine mate in the privacy of their nest box. I know this for a fact because there have been a few occasions when I have peeped inside the nest box and accidentally caught them in the act. I gently closed the nest box and let them continue with their business.

Usually, when a pair is getting ready to go to nest, they start to spend a lot of time in the nest box during the day. The hen starts to rearrange the shavings in the nest box and make a concave impression in the shavings, or she may even kick most of the shavings right out

the entrance hole. If she kicks out all the shavings, it is advisable to replace the nest box with a deeper one. Otherwise, when she lays her eggs on the bottom of the empty nest box, they may crack.

Just before the hen lays an egg, her lower abdomen in the vent area will swell and appear to contain a lump (which is the egg). She should then lay her first egg within five days. She will spend most of the day in the nest box, making preparations for the clutch to come.

I have found that every pair of conures, regardless of species, acts somewhat differently when it comes to incubating eggs. Usually the hen does most of the incubating. Some hens start to incubate right away with the first egg, while others start after the third egg is laid. You will find that each hen has her own way of tending to her eggs. The hen will sometimes pluck feathers from her breast and abdomen when she is incubating eggs. This is done to warm the eggs better and, sometimes, to line the nest with feathers.

During this time the male usually stands guard outside the nest box. But some males may

help incubate the eggs or will just keep the hen company in the box. For example, I have a pair of Jandaya Conures that have nested many times. Not once has this male gone into the nest box to keep the hen company or help with the eggs. Another pair have also nested quite a few times. Each time this hen has laid eggs, the male has stayed in the nest box with her most of the day and all of the night.

I have a pair of Peach-fronted Conures that tend their eggs differently than any other pair of conures I've ever owned. The hen will go into the nest box and lay her eggs, but the male will do all the incubating. You will see the hen out all day; she enters the nest box only at night. The male comes out just to eat or bathe. Only after the hen has finished laying her clutch of eggs will she help the male with some of the incubating. When the eggs hatch, both brood and feed the chicks.

It is very hard to predict how many eggs will be laid. I have had clutches range from a single egg to as many as seven. Eggs also vary in size from species to species. I have found with my

Above, left: Sun Conure eggs. Jandaya, Gold-cap, and Nanday eggs are also about this size. *Right:* Candling over a flashlight shows the developing blood vessels in a fertile egg.

Facing page, top: Two Jandaya chicks just hatched from a clutch of six. *Middle:* Sun Conure, 6 days old. *Bottom:* The 6-day-old Sun Conure with another, 5 weeks old.

pairs that the little *Pyrrhura* conures lay large eggs, almost as big as the Jandaya, Sun, Nanday, and Golden-capped conures. My Cactus Conures laid and hatched eggs that were smaller than Cockatiel eggs. The incubation period for conure eggs also seems to vary somewhat, with the average being twenty-five days. I have had eggs hatch as early as twenty-two days and as late as twenty-eight days after the start of incubation.

Candling Eggs If an egg is fertile, it will darken to a solid white color and will no longer have a transparent look. If you want to see whether the eggs are fertile, you can candle the eggs when they have been under the hen for about eight days, or a couple of days sooner if they have been in an incubator. To make your own candler, take a bright flashlight and cover the whole of the lens with aluminum foil. Then take a pencil and make a hole in the foil, about the same diameter as the pencil. Turn on the flashlight and carefully hold the egg over the hole in the foil. If the egg is fertile, you will see dark veins in the egg. If it is getting close to hatching, it will not be transparent; all it will have is an air space on the large end of the egg. This candling procedure should be done in a semidark place. As time goes on, you will not need to candle eggs to tell if they are fertile. The more clutches of eggs you have seen, the more experience you will gain. Soon you'll be able to distinguish fertile from infertile eggs when they are in the nest box. If an egg is fertile but has not hatched, you can candle the egg to see if the chick is still alive and moving. A candler can be convenient to have on hand.

Egg Binding The term *egg binding* means that the hen cannot pass her egg. Her vent area will be swollen with a lump, which is the egg that cannot be pushed out. The hen will have fluffed feathers, look sick, and not be inclined to fly. She will also appear very weak, with her eyes partially shut. The hen may come out of the nest box, or she may stay inside trying to pass the egg, until she is totally exhausted and dies. This can happen with any egg in the clutch, and it can happen with any clutch.

Egg binding usually occurs when a hen has not received enough vitamin D or calcium in her diet. It can also happen to immature or overbred hens. There are many other possible reasons why this happens. It is very important that conure hens be in top condition before attempting to breed them.

If you find an egg-bound hen, she should be treated immediately. Warm some mineral oil or olive oil. With an eyedropper, carefully insert a drop or two into her vent. Do not insert the eyedropper too far; if the egg is broken, the hen may die. Next, hold the hen for a few minutes with her vent about eight inches away from the steam of a tea kettle or a pot of boiling water. Then put her into a small cage with no perches. A heating pad under the cage should be set on Low to Medium. She should pass the egg within a few hours. After the egg has been laid, she can be returned to her mate and nest box, with the egg. Be sure to watch the hen very carefully to see that this does not happen again. If so, the whole procedure must be repeated.

One of my hens became egg-bound, and no matter what I did, she could not pass her egg.

The worst thing was that it was a Sunday, and I could not get in touch with a vet. By that evening, the hen was hemorrhaging through her vent. There was literally a puddle of blood in the cage. I contacted a good friend, Frank Lanier, who knew birds (inside and out), and brought the hen to him. He heated up a tea kettle and held her with her vent over the steam. By this time the bird was no longer moving and appeared to be dead. As he held her over the steam, he started to gently move the egg inside her. He found that the egg was turned sideways. He rotated the egg, and out it popped, whole and in perfect condition. The hen was still not moving. I gave her some thin, warm baby formula and honey very carefully with an eyedropper and put her into a cage with a heating pad underneath. In a couple of hours she revived. The next day she was returned to her aviary and nest box with her egg. She hatched out her clutch and has been fine ever since!

If you cannot get the hen to expel the egg, the best thing is to consult your veterinarian or an experienced bird breeder.

Unhatched Fertile Eggs

You cannot expect every egg in a clutch to hatch, even if they are all fertile. Even under natura conditions not all the eggs in every nest hatch.

There are many reasons why all fertile eggs do not hatch. One of the most common is that the birds had been off their nest. Many birds that have been scared off their nest return soon to continue to incubate their eggs. But if this occurred during the night, they may have waited till daylight to return to the nest box. If the pair returned to the eggs in the early morning, you

66

Slender-billed Conure pair. While their slender bills are apparently adapted to extracting the nuts of the monkey-puzzle tree, our birds have used them to open every kind of latch we've put on their cages. So far they've been defeated only by padlocks. We've also noticed that they are not particularly inclined to chew wood.

would have no idea that anything had gone wrong. But unfortunately, if it was a cold night, by morning the embryos could have chilled and died.

Also, some pairs of conures do not incubate properly. If there have been distractions close by, they may have kept leaving the nest box to see what the commotion was. Other pairs just do not have their hearts into raising a family yet. Many times very young birds do not settle down and incubate properly.

If you have a pair of conures that have nested three times, with most of the eggs fertile, but did not hatch any, it would be advisable to have a vet run cultures on the parents and the eggs. One or both of the pair could be a carrier of some sort of infection which could be passed on to the eggs, killing the embryos before they hatch. If this turns out to be the case and

the birds are treated, the pair will probably hatch the next clutch. (Everything must also be cleaned and disinfected, of course.)

There are times when everything seems to be going just fine, but one or two fertile eggs do not hatch. This could be caused by a cracked egg, or the shell may have been porous. Such eggs may become infected, or they simply could have dried up.

It is very important that breeding conures receive calcium in some form (cuttlebone, mineral block, or vitamins) to ensure that the shells on the eggs will be strong. Inadequate nutrition might cause the chick to be too weak to hatch, or even be deformed or underdeveloped.

Sometimes, especially in the hot summer months, the nest box can become too dry. The birds must be given water to bathe, so their eggs can be kept moist and humid. Otherwise, the shells could become too dry and hard for the chicks to break through. Also, without enough moisture in the nest box, the eggs could dry out long before they are ready to hatch.

Just remember, not every egg will hatch, even though the conures are cared for properly. We can only do our best and let nature take its course (with a little help, maybe).

Inspecting the Nest Box In my opinion, it is very important to inspect the nest box daily when the conures are starting to go to nest. If you make this part of your daily routine, the birds will become accustomed to this nest box check. The reason the nest box should be checked daily is to make sure the hen, eggs, and babies are doing fine.

Sometimes a hen will become egg-bound. If she is left unattended, she may die. You can also check how the incubation is proceeding. Freshly laid eggs look transparent, with a pinkish cast to them. Fertile eggs will start to darken and appear solid white. Also, the egg will darken if it has been cracked or dried out.

While inspecting the nest box, you may find a cracked egg; if it's found in time, you may be able to repair it. If there is a small crack, you can try to seal it with a coat or two of nail polish, just on the crack. When the nail polish is completely dry (in about five minutes), the egg should be returned to the nest box. If the egg is placed in the box before the polish is dry, the egg may get nesting material stuck to it, or it may stick to the hen and get broken.

On inspection you can also see if the hen has stopped incubating or started to break

Above: Hinged lids make nest-box inspection easy. If your conures are accustomed to this practice, there's no danger they will desert the nest.

Facing page: Conures at 4 weeks of age: Nanday (*top*), Dusky-headed (*middle*), Peach-fronted (*bottom*).

68

her eggs. If so, they should be removed immediately and placed in an incubator or under another hen which has eggs at about the same stage of incubation.

After the first pip, a chick can take up to forty-eight hours to hatch. If a chick gets stuck in the egg, you can help to remove it —but this situation occurs very rarely if the conures are incubating the eggs. If the hen has been provided with water for bathing, the shell usually will not be too hard or dry for the chick to hatch out.

Once the chicks hatch, you should keep a close watch on the hatchlings, to make sure the hen is feeding them. If, for some reason, she quits feeding, the chicks should be removed for hand-feeding. Some pairs start to pick on their chicks for one reason or another. Sometimes the pair wants to go back to nest or just wants their babies out. All chicks should be removed immediately to be hand-fed if there is any sign of blood on them. This is a warning that if the chicks are left in the nest box, they could be killed by their parents at any time.

Keep an eye on the nest box for holes. I had a pair gnaw a hole in the box while nesting. Instead of changing the nest box, I covered the hole with welded wire. I cut a piece of ¼-inch mesh a little larger than the hole and stapled it to the outside. I then covered the wire with many layers of masking tape so it would be dark inside and look like wood. If the nest box had been changed, the birds more than likely would have deserted their eggs.

If you will be checking the nest box while the hen is inside, try not to chase her out of the box. It should only take a few seconds to check on the eggs or

chicks. There is no need to
touch them unless you suspect a
problem. Usually conures do just
fine with their eggs and babies,
and very few problems arise.

Helping a Chick Hatch It
can take up to forty-eight hours
for a chick to free itself from the
shell. During the last hours the
chick is absorbing the remainder
of the yolk sac, which contains
the food that fed the chick until
it was ready to hatch. Once the
yolk sac has been completely

absorbed, the chick will hatch,
and not before. If the chick is
helped out before it is ready to
hatch, it will die. So before ever
helping a chick hatch, be sure
that the eggshell has been
pipped for over twenty-four
hours.

The chick starts to pip at the
large end of the eggshell, using
its egg tooth, which is on the tip
of the upper mandible..
Sometimes the membrane in the
egg dries out and sticks to the
chick. This may make the chick

Mitred Conures, adult
pair. Because it's very
hard to tell which bird is
which, both were tattooed
on the underside of the
wing web after surgical
sexing—males on the right,
females on the left.

70

Red-masked Conure young. *Right:* Nine days previously this chicked hatched from an egg like the one shown beside it. *Below, left:* 5-week-old chick. *Right:* 9-week-old chick. At this stage the only red feathering is under the wings; red will begin to appear on the head when it is about 5 months old.

unable to finish the hatching process of extending its head and neck and freeing itself from the shell. The chick is a prisoner inside and will surely die.

If the chick cannot free itself, you can try to help. If any bleeding should occur while you are helping the chick out of its shell, you must stop instantly and put the egg in an incubator. If the chick has not hatched out on its own, you can try again in a few hours.

Very carefully, with a toothpick, pick off bits of the shell at the large end of the egg, where it is pipped, slowly, around the egg. Watch where the chick is inside the shell, and be very careful not to poke the chick with the toothpick. Do not pick at the shell surrounding the chick, below where it has been pipped. Dampen the membrane with a slightly wet cotton swab and slowly remove the top (the large end) of the eggshell. Do not get water on the chick's face, or it may drown. After this is done, you should put the egg, with the chick still inside, in an incubator and let the chick free itself. This is just in case the chick needs a few more hours in the egg. After the chick has emerged, it should be returned to its parents. If it is to be hand-fed, it should be left in the incubator, with the first feeding being about six hours from the time of hatching. The temperature should be dropped to between 95 and 98 F.

Using Incubators It is a very good idea to have an incubator on hand when you are breeding conures, just in case an emergency arises. You just never know what is going to happen when birds go to nest. Occasionally problems do arise: a hen could abandon her eggs

Left: Pipped Sun Conure egg. The top of the beak is visible. *Right:* The hole is enlarged with a toothpick, around the egg at the point where it has been pipped.

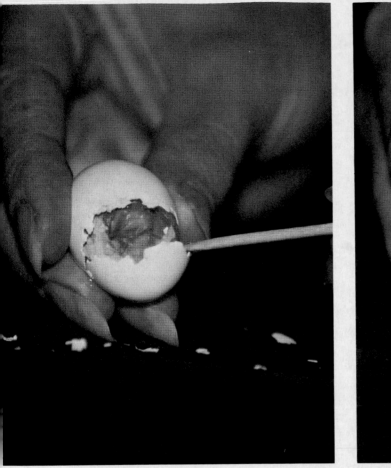 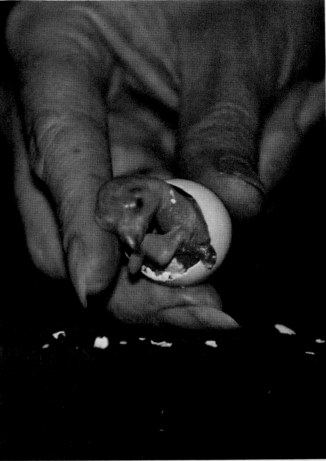

Left: The end of the egg shell is pulled away. *Right:* The chick's head and right wing emerged at once.

or even die unexpectedly while incubating. The eggs can then be temporarily placed in the incubator till a foster hen that is on eggs is located. Or the eggs could even be left in the incubator till they hatch and the chicks then be hand-fed.

Sometimes the hen gets off the babies for one reason or another. If the babies are left unattended for too long, they may become chilled. If these babies are placed in an incubator, they will warm up instantly and usually be just fine. I had a chick once that appeared to be dead. It had apparently crawled away from its nestmates and ended up in a corner of the nest box, where it spent the night. When I found the chick in the early morning, it looked frozen. With close examination, it was apparent that it was still breathing. I immediately placed it in an incubator, and soon the

chick "thawed out" and came to life. So please check all "dead" babies over carefully before tossing them out.

I use a small dome-type incubator that can be purchased inexpensively. I particularly like the clear plastic dome through which the eggs and chicks can be observed. I keep three of these incubators on hand in case, for some reason, one will not operate properly and because they can also be used for brooding chicks. The temperature in these incubators can easily and quickly be adjusted; at a touch the temperature can be dropped and the incubator used as a brooder for a new-born or very young chick.

I have found that keeping the temperature set between 99.4 and 100.5 F. is good for hatching eggs. Water must be in the incubator at all times, for proper

73

humidity. With this type of incubator I keep the tray full of water all the time eggs are inside.

The eggs must be turned at least three times a day. When the eggs are under the hen, she turns them with her beak many times a day, so the embryos will develop properly. If the eggs are not turned often enough, the chicks may be born with leg or foot disorders or they may even be too weak to hatch. The more you turn them—up to six times during a twenty-four hour period —the better for the embryo. Once you hear or see the chick hatching, turning the egg should be discontinued.

Any incubator that does not fluctuate in temperature will do the job. An incubator is not a big expense, and after saving just one baby it has paid for itself and then some. I have found it to be a necessary and very good investment when raising conures.

The Growing Chicks There is nothing more beautiful than the hatching of your first new-born chick. Conure chicks are totally helpless and for quite a while will be completely dependent on their parents, or on humans, if a problem should arise. The hatchlings are a pink color, sparsely covered in an off-white down, which later will fall off. Their eyes are closed and will not start to open till they are about twelve days old. When the chicks are twelve to fourteen days old, the dark feather sheaths developing under the skin will become visible. At this age, the chicks also start to develop pigment in the beak, cere, and feet.

At fifteen days old, the second coat of down starts to appear. By the time the chicks reach twenty-one days, they are

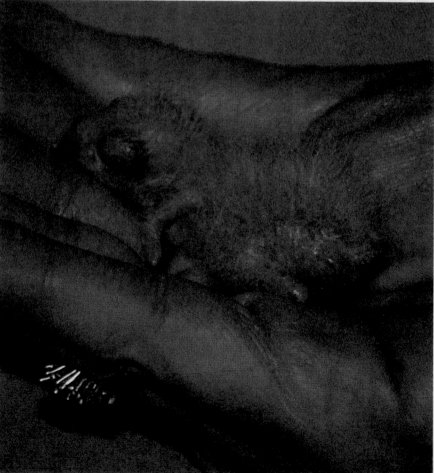

Right: Jandaya Conure chicks—16 and 17 days old (*top*); 4 weeks old (*middle*); 5 weeks old (*bottom*).

Facing page: Jandaya Conure chick—just hatched in an incubator (*top*), and 4 days old (*bottom*).

covered with down, with feather sheaths underneath. The second down is very thick, making the chicks look like big, round, fuzzy balls. Depending on the species of conure, the second layer of down varies in color. Sun Conure chicks have a light yellow color. Jandaya Conures have a grayish white down, while Maroon-bellied and Golden-capped conures have a gray-colored down. My Cactus Conure chicks never developed a thick second layer of down. They remained somewhat naked, compared to other species.

At about twenty-three days old, some colored feathers are "popping" through the sheaths on the wings, shoulders, tail, and top of the head. By the time the chicks reach five weeks of age, most of their feathers have come through the sheaths and fanned open, though much

down is still left. But there are some chicks that at this age still have that quilly, "porcupine" look to them. Most of the unopened feathers are on the back of the neck, breast, under the wings, and on the back and face. When the chicks are seven weeks old, they are almost completely covered with feathers, but some down will remain under their wings for quite a few weeks. This is how they look when, in another week or so, they fledge—if you have left the chicks to be raised by the parents, that is.

Keeping Records   It is vitally important to keep records on every pair of birds you own. About some things you can make a mental note, but once you have quite a few birds, it is necessary to keep some sort of log. This can be done in a note-book or even on a calendar.

Peach-front nestmates, 19 to 26 days old.

76

Sun Conures, 11 weeks old, all from the same brood. It will take about two years for them to attain full adult coloration.

There are many reasons for keeping written records. You can go back in your notes and see how a pair of birds cared for their eggs and chicks. You can see whether they incubated their eggs well, fed their young, or plucked their babies' feathers. If a pair has fostered eggs or chicks, this too should be kept on record. Whatever else you may need to know should also be written down. It is easy to think that if you do not write it down, you will remember; but as time goes on, you will forget some things. If you have several pairs of birds, you can easily mix up your mental information about which birds did what.

Some things should be recorded for each pair of birds: how many eggs were laid in a clutch, and at what intervals; how many were fertile and hatched; the incubation period of the eggs; how the babies

developed; how well the parents fed the chicks; and when the babies fledged and became independent. Other notes can also be taken, such as: what size of cage or aviary was used for breeding; what kind of nest box was used; what foods the pair ate; which parents incubated the eggs; how many chicks hatched and lived—and whatever else you may want to know in the future.

If you are having a problem (for example) with a pair of conures that will not feed their young, by keeping a log you will know if this pair have done this in the past, with other broods. This way you will be prepared to take action when the young hatch, or you may even decide to break up the pair and give them different mates. When you are raising birds, some problems do arise. A written record will help you be prepared for them.

Slender-billed Conures, *Enicognathus leptorhynchus*, adult pair.

Rearing Chicks

Rearing by Parents   Most conures are excellent parents and don't have any problems when it comes to hatching, feeding, and brooding their young, provided they are housed adequately and are fed a good, nutritious diet. In most cases, both parents tend their chicks, but I do have a few pairs in which the hen does all the brooding and feeding of the young, while the male stands guard outside the nest box.

Once the chicks have hatched, the parent birds are very protective. Many hens often spread their wings and cover their babies when you look inside the nest box. Some hens will even rock up and down or from side to side and growl to keep you away from the young. This is how they protect their chicks. If you try to stick your hand in the nest box, you will more than likely be severely bitten. If the chicks are moving and look fine, I leave well enough alone and let nature take its course.

If the first baby that hatched should die and apparently was not fed (you can see no food in the crop), I then keep a very close watch on the chicks that are still hatching. If these are also not fed, they are removed from the nest box and are either hand-fed or placed under another pair of conures that have babies of about the same age.

There are times when a hen will feed all her chicks except for one, which she will throw out or move to the opposite corner of the nest box, to be left to die. It is very possible that she knows best—there may be something physically wrong with the chick. I had a Jandaya Conure hen that refused to feed one of her chicks; all she did was to move it to another part of the nest box. I kept putting it back, and she kept pushing it out from under her. She continued to feed and care for her other chicks but not this one. I tried using various proven foster parents, but all of them refused to care for and feed this particular chick. So I decided to hand-feed it. After about three weeks it died; the chick just never grew. I am now sure that the hen knew something was very wrong with the chick, and that's why nobody wanted it.

Usually Nature does know best, but not always. Another time that I had the same problem, I hand-fed the baby chick, and it grew up to be healthy and just fine. All I am saying here is, if you try to save a chick and it does not live, it may have had something wrong internally from the time of birth. It is very important you realize that all you can do is your very best.

If there is ever any sign of blood on the chicks, they must be removed and placed under another hen or hand-fed. There have been instances where injuries were inflicted on one chick by one of its nestmates. Baby conure chicks at three weeks of age can already inflict a very powerful bite with their strong beaks. I have myself had to separate chicks from one another for fear that one would become severely injured or even killed by a nestmate. Keep in mind that this situation is very rare but does occasionally happen. Most of the time, if the chicks have been plucked, it's being done by their parents. Sometimes the parents want to start another clutch of eggs, so they try to throw the babies out of the nest. Or they may just pluck the feathers from the chicks' backs, or even go as far as killing their chicks. Since you can't be sure what may happen, chicks must be removed at the first sign of any blood.

Fostering Foster parents, if available, can be a lifesaver for young chicks. You can place an abandoned chick or two into a nest of other youngsters, but you must keep a very close watch on them. It is advisable that you check the chick added to the nest about fifteen minutes after placing it there. This is to see if the hen has accepted the new baby and included it with her other chicks. If not, she will refuse to brood it and will push it out from under her. When this happens, you must remove the chick immediately, or she may kill it. But if you find that she is brooding the chick with her

Above: Maroon-bellied
Conures *Pyrrhura frontalis
chiripepe*, 4 to 5 weeks old.

Facing page, top: Peach-
front, 26 days old. At any
age Peach-fronts vary
considerably from one to
the next in the amount of
orange on the forehead.
Middle: Jandaya
nestmates, both 10 weeks
old. Note the difference in
appearance. *Bottom:* The
Yellow-collared Macaw,
Ara auricollis, 5 weeks old,
is one of three fostered to
the parents of the Blue-
crowned Conure, 6 weeks
old, which is also one of a
brood of three. The Blue-
crowned adults fed all six
for two weeks, until they
were removed for hand-
rearing.

others, then it is more than likely
that all will be well. Still, I would
advise that you check the nest a
few more times during the day
to make sure everything is going
just fine with all the chicks.

When you need to foster, you
should select, from the pairs
which have chicks of their own,
whichever pair are the best
parents. By this I mean the pair
of conures that brood and feed
their chicks well, raising
beautiful, healthy babies.

Before placing any chick in
with foster parents, the main
thing to remember is that the
chick must be about the same
age as the babies already in the
nest. If the chick to be fostered
is about the same age as the
others, it will usually be accepted
by the foster parents quite
readily. If the foster baby is
much older than their own
chicks, they may not feed it. On
the other hand, if the baby is too

young, it may get trampled by
the other chicks and never have
a chance to live. But even if the
right situation isn't available (and
hand-feeding cannot be done), I
would then try anything to save
a chick. Just remember, a pair
of conures that do not have
babies at the time will not foster
any chick given to them.

Also, it is desirable if, for
example, you can put Jandaya
Conure chicks under Jandaya
Conure foster parents. But I
know this is not always possible.
I have had *Pyrrhura* parents
feed *Aratinga* conure babies,
and vice versa. For example, I
had a pair of Maroon-bellied
Conures feed a baby Cactus
Conure when they already had
five Maroon-bellied chicks of
their own to care for. A pair of
my Green-cheeked Conures
fostered a Nanday chick, and a
pair of Cactus Conures fed
Maroon-bellied chicks. I even

had a pair of Cockatiels feed a Jandaya chick; at the time no nesting conures had babies about the same age as the Jandaya chick.

Reasons for Hand-Rearing

There are various reasons why you may have to hand-raise baby conure chicks. It may be that the parents abandoned the eggs or chicks, and no foster parents were available at the time. Maybe the conure parents did not feed their youngsters well. Or the parents may have started to pluck the babies' feathers. Some people hand-feed to raise more babies from their birds. Others may just want very tame and lovable pet conures.

If you want to remove young chicks to hand-rear as tame pets, and the parents are doing a fine job with them, take them out at about three weeks of age. This way, the chicks have had a very good start with their parents. Also, it is much easier for you to hand-feed at this age, because the chicks will need to be fed only four times a day. I have found that at three weeks old, the chicks become accustomed to hand-feeding after just one or two feedings. If you wait and remove the chicks when they are much older, they will not take to hand-feeding so readily, and you will have to struggle with them for a couple of days till they get used to the hand-feeding procedure.

Once you decide to hand-feed, you must know that you are committed to give the best attention and care to the babies at all times! I kid you not—it is time consuming and may even be exhausting to feed a new-born chick every two hours around the clock, throughout the night, for the first week. But there is nothing more

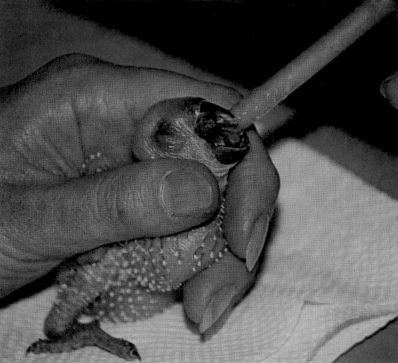

rewarding than seeing a beautiful, tame, and loving feathered creature learning to eat seeds on its own—and knowing that you raised it from a chick and nurtured a life!

Preparing to Hand-Rear

When breeding conures, you should be prepared to hand-feed chicks at any time. You never know when problems will arise, and by being prepared, you can act quickly to save a young chick's life. You should always have on hand the following: (1) a brooder; (2) a plastic eyedropper or pipette; (3) a jar of Gerber Rice Cereal (with applesauce and bananas).

When hand-feeding my baby conure chicks, I use a small cardboard box or a five-gallon aquarium as a brooder. Either one will do quite well, and each has its advantages. The cardboard box must be clean

and free from any odor. When the babies have outgrown the box, it can simply be tossed out in the garbage. This keeps any illness from spreading from one group of babies to another. Many people use a wooden box with a heating element and a thermostat installed, such as an incubator has. The wooden-box brooder is good, but I feel that it is very hard to sterilize wood completely and make it disease-free. The aquarium has advantages which I particularly like. In a clean glass aquarium, you can observe the chicks and the thermometer at all times. After the chicks are moved into a cage, the aquarium can be soaked in a disinfectant and washed and dried out thoroughly.

When preparing a box or aquarium for use as a brooder, I line the bottom with paper towels, and then I put in a one-inch layer of pine shavings. The shavings give the babies a stable footing, so straddle-leg will not develop. (In straddle-leg, the legs do not develop properly but spread out to the sides.) When the shavings become damp and soiled, the box should be cleaned out and fresh shavings added.

I next wrap a heating pad once with a small bath towel. Three-quarters of the box is placed on the heating pad, and the pad is turned on to the Medium setting. By placing three-quarters of the box on the heating pad, the baby chicks can move off the heated part of the box if they feel too warm. If the babies want more heat, they will move some of the shavings and lie closer to the bottom of the box, nearer the heat. The box is covered with a towel, except for about one inch left uncovered for fresh air. With this arrangement, the babies can keep themselves as warm as they like, more or less.

If the babies are too warm, they will sit up and pant. If this is the case, the heat in the brooder must be reduced till the babies seem comfortable. You can reduce the heat by wrapping another layer of the towel around the heating pad or by moving the box half-way off the pad. Babies in a brooder should feel warm to the touch. If they feel cool, the heat should be raised a little till they feel warmer.

I keep a thermometer in the box so I can read the temperature at any time. For chicks up to ten days old, I keep the brooder at about 95° F.; chicks ten days to four weeks old are kept at about 85° F. If there are two or more chicks in the brooder, when the babies are about four weeks old, and provided the temperature in the house does not drop below

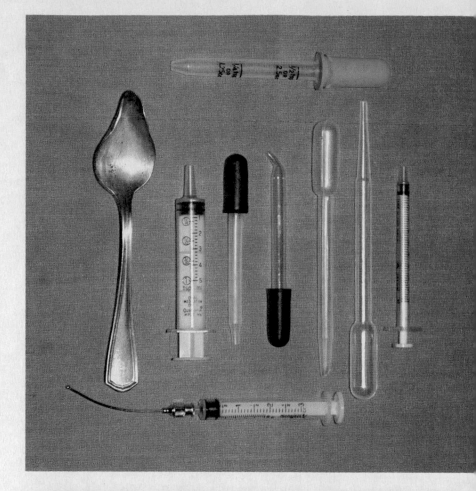

84

Above: Green-cheeked, Peach-fronted, Sun, and Rose-ringed Parakeet chicks, 11 to 16 days old. While these have just been removed for hand-rearing, their younger nestmates have been left in the nest, to be fed by their parents a while longer.

Facing page, top: Various implements for hand-rearing. *Below:* Hand-reared Maroon-bellied chick, 25 days old.

70° F., the heating pad can be turned off during the day and turned on to the Low setting at night. But if there is only one chick in the brooder, then the heating pad should be kept on the Low setting during the day and on the Medium setting at night. One chick by itself could easily chill if it got too cool in the house, for it would have nobody to cuddle up with to get warmer.

Once the babies become fully feathered, they no longer need the heating pad to keep them warm. They will soon be ready to be moved to a cage.

A baby conure will sleep on its stomach, side, and sometimes even on it back (and look dead at first sight). When I first started hand-feeding baby conures, there were times that I would find them lying on their backs, with their feet in the air. I would

grab the box in a panic and just about frighten the peacefully sleeping babies to death!

A chick's weight gain can be checked with a gram scale. By weighing the chicks every few days, you can see if they are gaining weight and growing. When you are feeding and seeing a chick continuously, it will sometimes seem that it's not growing. By weighing the chick, you can keep track of the weight gain and know how well the chick is doing. Here are some weights of chicks:

Nanday Conures weigh about 40 grams when 9 days old, 60 grams at 15 days, 70 grams at 18 days, and about 120 grams at 6 weeks.

Jandaya Conures weigh about 55 grams when 17 days old, 60 grams at 19 days, and about 105 grams at 6 weeks. The weights, of course, will vary a

little from chick to chick.

While there are many ways to hand-feed baby chicks, I prefer to use a plastic eyedropper or pipette. Either one can be cut at the tip to feed a larger chick more easily and rapidly. I also feel that with an eye dropper I have more control over how much food is fed to each chick. Other tools which can be used for hand-feeding are a syringe or a spoon with the sides bent up so the food will run straight down the spoon and not off the sides. You should use what is most comfortable for you.

There are times when baby conures are violent to each other, or maybe just one baby becomes dominant over the others. Usually the chicks are about four weeks of age when this happens. If so, they must be separated or they may become badly injured. (Sometimes when you are hand-feeding a chick, it will grab your finger if it is very hungry, and you can feel what a strong and powerful grip it has at even this very young age.) Once the babies are about nine weeks old, they can be put back together again, and usually everything will be peaceful. I am not sure why some babies behave so violently toward others, but this may be the reason why I have heard many breeders say that all the babies in the nest were fine one day, but the next day all were dead except for one chick. I too have had it happen that I would find one baby all bruised and beaten up. It would be hard to say whether the parents or an older nestmate did it. Keep in mind that while this happens only on rare occasions, it *can* happen.

Hand-rearing Schedule If a baby conure hatched in an incubator is going to be hand-

Left: During hand-rearing, chicks should be weighed each day, like this 15-day-old Green-cheek, since daily weight gain is a sign of good health. *Right:* As the Peach-front and the Senegal grow and become better able to maintain body temperature, the heat in the brooder can be reduced by adjusting the thermostat of the heating pad.

86

Feeding time for some chicks. One hand must always be firmly on the chick, at all times!

fed, it is best if you wait approximately six hours before it receives its first feeding. This will ensure that it has absorbed most of the yolk sac, which is what the chick feeds on until it hatches. The first feeding should consist of a very thin (souplike) cereal.

After each feeding, it is very important to clean the chick's face and beak. If this is not done right away, the cereal could harden and cause mouth sores or even beak deformity.

My baby conures one to three days old receive a couple of

drops at each feeding, by eyedropper, of Gerber Rice Cereal (with applesauce and bananas). A small amount is warmed up and thinned with some water. I test this on my upper lip. If it feels warm—not hot—it is immediately fed to the chick, before it cools. If the food is too cold, the chick will be unable to digest it and more than likely will develop sour crop. Sometimes a couple of drops of blackstrap molasses or a pinch of baking soda added to some very thin, warm cereal can help relieve this problem. You

should also massage the crop each time the baby is fed, till all the undigested food has been completely absorbed. It is much easier to prevent sour crop than to cure it.

The young chick receives this prepared cereal for the first three days and is fed every two hours around the clock, provided the crop is empty. As the crop of a chick is transparent, you can see the food inside. Do not overfeed the chick; it is better to feed too little than too much. If the chick is overfed, the crop may become impacted or sour crop may develop. During each feeding the chick is very excited. Many of them will bob their heads with great force. You should hold onto the chick's head with your thumb and forefinger on each side by the ear hole, keeping the chick's head up while it's being fed. You must hold onto the chick's body and head so that it

will not injure itself while being fed. Also, make sure you hold onto the eyedropper securely, because a three-week-old chick can force the eyedropper down its throat and hurt itself.

The chick should be placed in a bowl when being hand-fed so it will not crawl off the table and fall on the floor. You should have one hand on the chick at all times. Believe me, they are squirmy little things.

When the chick is three days old, I add some of my own cooked formula to the Rice Cereal (I'll give the recipe later on). Very slowly I change over to my formula, and by the time the chick is fourteen days old, it will be old enough to be fed on my formula alone, without the Rice Cereal.

When a chick is being hand-fed from hatching, it will not always develop the "friendly bacteria" needed to break down

Usually, chicks of different species can be kept together for hand-rearing, provided they are about the same age. These are Peach-fronts, Green-cheeks, and Jandays, about 4 to 5 weeks old.

Jandaya nestmates, 9
weeks old—a further
illustration of the
individual variation that
may be expected in
species showing a lot of
yellow-to-red coloration.

food. If this is the case, the chick
may stop digesting its food when
it is around a week old. To avert
this, I use yogurt to furnish the
bacteria to help the chick digest
its food. Some people use a
pinch of powdered acidophilus
or a drop of two of acidophilus
liquid in a couple of feedings,
instead of yogurt—either will
work. However, if the parent
birds have fed the chick for even
a day, they more than likely
passed on the bacteria needed
for digestion via the regurgitated
food. In this case, the yogurt will
not be necessary.

I start to add a little yogurt to
the formula at one or two
feedings when the chick is about
one week old. I will repeat the
yogurt two more times, at about
ten days old and again at two
weeks.

When a chick is one to seven
days old, it should be fed about
every two hours. From seven to
fourteen days old, feedings
should be about every three to
four hours, depending on how
fast the chick digests its food.
From two to four weeks old, it
should be fed four times a day.
Between four weeks and eight
weeks of age, reduce feedings to
three times a day.

Once the chick is fully
feathered (around eight weeks
old), it is placed into a cage and
fed twice a day until it is
weaned.

The first food that a chick
should be offered to eat on its
own—in the cage—should be
bread, apple, peas, corn, and
water. After about a week in the
cage, the chick can be offered
sunflower seed, safflower seed,
and budgie mix as well. When
the chick starts to eat on its
own, you need hand-feed it only
once a day, in the evening
before bedtime, which ensures
enough food to get the chick

through the night. Once the chick is cracking seed and eating fruits and vegetables, it is on its own. When I am about to discontinue hand-feeding entirely, and afterwards for about a week, I check to make sure the chick is eating well by feeling its crop.

In hand-rearing, I have had few problems weaning the babies. Once in a great while I will run into one that does not want to be weaned as soon as others. All I can do is offer it

Blue-crowned Conures, 9 weeks old, in a cage for weaning. The wire floor helps keep the chicks clean.

Sun Conure siblings, 8 weeks old, just starting to eat on their own.

seeds, fruits, and vegetables while continuing to hand-feed it twice a day.

Pyrrhura chicks grow at a faster rate than the aratingas, so they start to eat on their own as early as eight weeks of age. Others take their time and wait until they are older. Almost all baby conures are weaned by the time they are twelve weeks old, however. But no two chicks develop at exactly the same pace, no matter what species they are. It is very important that

each baby is treated as an individual!

Formula for Hand-rearing The hand-feeding formula I use can be made in advance and stored for five days in the refrigerator or for six months in the freezer.

    5 cups water
    1 cup quick oatmeal
    ½ cup wheat hearts
    ½ cup high-protein baby
        cereal
    ½ teaspoon salt
    1 tablespoon corn oil
    1 tablespoon honey

Add salt, oil, honey, and the cereals to the water, stirring continuously to prevent lumps. After the cereal has cooked (three to five minutes after it boils), remove the pot from the stove and add:

    1 jar (4½ oz.) creamed
        spinach baby food
    1 jar (4½ oz.) strained peas
        baby food
    1 jar (4½ oz.) strained
        carrots baby food
    1 jar (4½ oz.) creamed
        corn baby food
    1 jar (4½ oz.)
        applesauce
    1 cup powdered milk
    2 cups sunflower meal

To prepare your own sunflower meal, put sunflower kernels into a blender along with dried wheat bread broken up into crumbs, and blend till very fine. The dried bread crumbs keep the sunflower kernels from becoming sticky.

After the formula is prepared, it must be stored in plastic containers in the refrigerator or freezer. I keep a small container in the refrigerator and warm up the amount of food needed at

Above: Some of the ingredients used in preparing my hand-rearing formula.

Facing page: Pet conures. *Top, left:* Even kept together in a cage as pet, the Red-masked male and the Nanday hen produced two fertile eggs, which, unfortunately, never hatched. *Top, right:* Sunny lives in a wrought-iron cage in our living room. *Bottom:* Young conures are very playful, much like puppies. These hand-reared, tame chicks—Peach-fronted, Jandaya, Nanday, Dusky-headed, Green-cheeked, and Sun—love to be out of their cage, playing and climbing on the playground.

each feeding. If there is any left after the chick has been fed, it is discarded. This formula may have to be thinned down with water at each feeding. I use a microwave oven to warm the formula, but a small pot on the stove could also be used. At one feeding each day, I add a drop or two of liquid vitamin complex to the formula. I prefer to use a good liquid vitamin because it seems to mix with the formula better than powder does. Every other day, I add a couple of drops of cod-liver oil to the formula at one feeding.

With proper care you should hand-raise many healthy, beautiful babies. All our conures do wonderfully on this formula. They are all big and healthy, and their feathers are strong and shiny.

There are many other formulas which could be used to hand-feed conure chicks successfully. For example, I have known many people to use a monkey chow (Zu/Preem Primate Dry) and powdered milk for their formula. The monkey chow is broken into small pieces and then put into a blender and ground till it becomes a fine powder. The powdered monkey chow is stored dry in a sealed container. At each feeding, some of the powdered monkey chow is put into a bowl and a small amount of powdered milk is added, to give the growing chicks calcium. Hot water is slowly added to the mixture of monkey chow and powdered milk, till it becomes a smooth, thin gruel. It is tested to make sure it is the proper temperature before it is fed to the chick. After the chick is fed, any leftover gruel is discarded. This is a much less complex formula, but I have heard nothing but excellent reports about it—all the chicks thrive and develop

Trimming the wing feathers of a tame young Jandaya Conure to restrict flight. Use scissors to cut about half off the primary feathers of both wings (*facing page*). The secondaries need not be clipped (*above*).

beautifully. This formula is also excellent if you are hand-feeding chicks while traveling.

Conures for Pets If the chicks are to be pets, their wings should be clipped when they are about eight weeks old. I prefer to clip both wings, so the bird will have balance if it should take a fall, and will be less likely to get hurt.

When selling a young conure for a pet, you should write out a basic instruction list specifying what it has been eating and what other accessories may be needed, such as mineral block and grit. The new owner will greatly appreciate this, and it will show that you really care for the well-being of the young conure.

As many people who purchase a conure for a pet may never have owned a bird before, this list will be very helpful, maybe even necessary. It is also a good idea if you give the new owner some of the seed the conure is used to. This will make the young bird more at ease with the change in surroundings—at least the food will still look the same. Sunflower seeds come not only in different sizes but also in different colors, such as gray-striped or black. The kind the new owner may be able to obtain may look strange to a young conure. All the changes could be very stressful, so every little bit of consideration can help the young conure adjust to its new home.

Green-cheeked Conures *Pyrrhura molinae molinae*, adult pair.

Breeding—
Case
Histories

The Green-cheeked Conure
Our introduction to conures
came several years ago, with
Sun Conures. For the greater
part of a year, we kept six Suns
for our friend, Frank Lanier, and
housed them in an aviary eight
feet high, three feet wide, and
eight feet long. The birds played
and enjoyed themselves the
whole while, but no breeding
occurred, though we believed
they were three pairs. This was
later confirmed when Frank took
them and bred them all,
separately in cages.

A pair of Patagonians were
the only conures we owned
when, on May 31, 1980, my
husband and I received another
little conure. At the time we
believed it to be a Maroon-
bellied. The poor thing was in
dreadfully bad shape, having no
flight or tail feathers, and also
most of its face feathers had
been rubbed off. The conure
was put into a Cockatiel cage in
the house. It was quite apparent
that this bird was very nervous,
for it would continue to rub its
head and face up and down on
the cage bars all day! After
watching the poor thing and its
very nervous state for two days,
we transferred it to a larger cage
outdoors, which had a standard
Cockatiel nest box attached to
the outside. The conure seemed

more content in this cage but
would hide in the nest box at
the first sight of us. Apparently
this bird needed some place to
retreat to for security, for the
nervous rubbing ceased.

This cage, set up with
separate feeders for sunflower
and safflower seeds and budgie
mix, with a crock for water, is
16 x 16 x 48 inches long. It is
located in a flight 8 x 8 x 6 feet
high, where it is one of nine
cages set up for breeding
psittacines.

About a month later, as the
conure's feathers started to fill
in, we discovered that it was
really a Green-cheeked Conure
(Pyrrhura molinae molinae).
Now that the conure was strong
and we knew exactly what kind
it was, we decided it was now
time to find out what sex it was.
Our vet surgically sexed it and
reported it was a very healthy,
mature hen. So we started our
search for a mate for her.

About the end of July 1980,
we spotted a Green-cheeked
Conure, in perfect feather, for
sale in a pet shop. My husband
checked it by the pelvic-bone
method and thought it was a
male. So we purchased the bird,
and home we went with high
hopes that we now owned a
pair. The next day we had our
vet surgically sex the new

*Fred and Robbie Harris received
1981 U. S. First Breeding Avy
Awards from the American
Federation of Aviculture for
their achievements with a
"Subspecies of the Green-
cheeked Conure (Pyrrhura
molinae molinae)" and with
the "Cactus Conure (Aratinga
cactorum cactorum)."*

conure, and he confirmed that it was a male, mature and in excellent health. He was introduced to the hen in her cage, and it was love at first sight. The two Green-cheeks seemed to be inseparable. They sat side by side preening each other, they ate together, and they also spent lots of time in the nest box together. There was no doubt that they were a compatible pair.

On January 14, 1981, we discovered an egg cushioned in pine shavings in the nest box. This was the third time a conure had laid eggs for us! By January 21, a total of four eggs had been laid. Both conures spent most of the day and the entire night in the nest box. They came out only to eat and bathe. I inspected the nest box every morning to make sure all was well. It was obvious about a week after the last egg was laid

that all four were fertile.

Inspecting the nest box on February 5, I discovered the first chick had started to pip. On February 7, the chick hatched. By February 11, all four chicks had hatched and all were doing just fine. The adults were excellent parents, always keeping their chicks warm and well fed. The hen left the nest box only to eat and bathe. The male also spent a lot of time in the nest box with the hen and chicks. The chicks progressed beautifully.

When the chicks were between two and three weeks of age, they were all removed for hand-feeding. All the chicks were doing just fine with their parents, but I personally prefer to remove conure chicks at this age and hand-feed. I find that hand-feeding produces calmer birds, whether for pets or breeding. Also, I didn't want to

Above: The Green-cheeks are kept in the lower cage; the upper cage houses the pair of Cactus Conures.

Facing page, top: One of the hand-reared Green-cheeked chicks from the second nesting, 6 weeks old. *Bottom:* The third brood of Green-cheeks; the youngest is 18 days old; the oldest, 27 days.

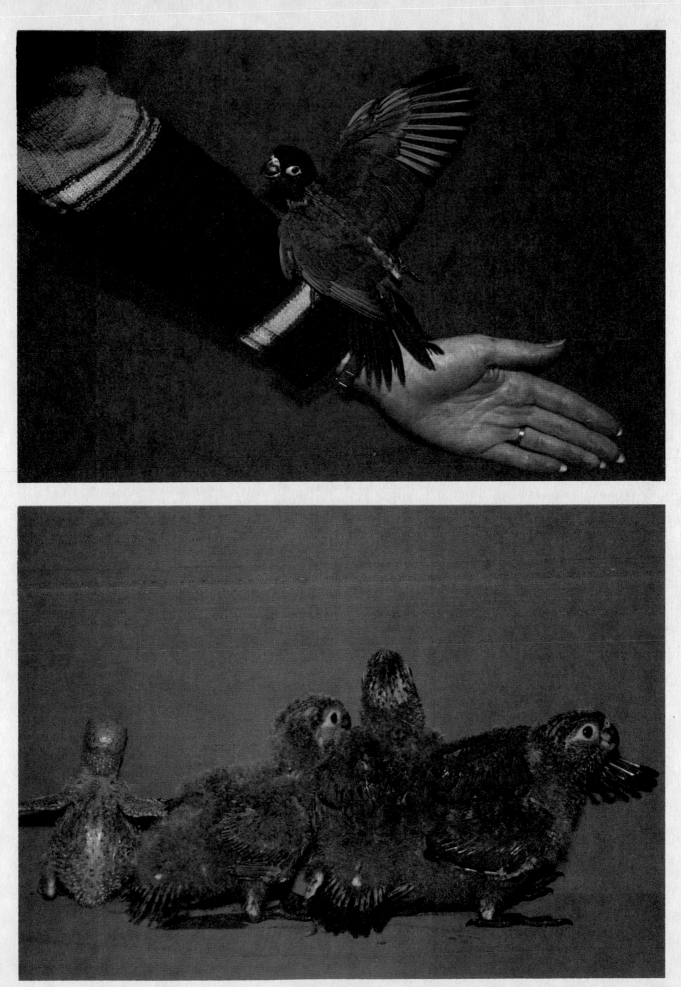

take any chances; in February, it can become quite cold during the night, and if the parents were scared off their nest and did not return to it, the chicks would chill and more than likely be dead by morning.

The four baby Green-cheeks were placed in a cardboard box which had a couple of layers of paper towels and about two inches of pine shavings on the bottom. Box and chicks were then put into our bird nursery. They were not alone! I was hand-feeding sixty-five baby birds at that time: five Maroon-bellied Conures, two orange-bellied Senegal Parrots, two golden-mantled Eastern Rosellas, one Andean Parakeet, one Rose-ringed Parakeet, two Barred Parakeets, Peach-Faced Lovebirds of all colors, and Cockatiels of all sorts. The formula I used for hand-feeding all these baby birds is the same one given earlier in this book.

The Green-cheeked chicks grew into beautiful, strong,

Besides the Green-cheeks *Pyrrhura molinae molinae*, we also keep the subspecies *restricta*. Shown here is an adult male.

Green-cheek *Pyrrhura molinae molinae*, 9 weeks old, another chick from the second nesting.

healthy birds. They were put into a cage when about six weeks old. By the time they were eight weeks old, they were eating sunflower seed, budgie mix, apples, oranges, peas, corn, and whole-wheat bread—they were independent, eating on their own.

The young conures resembled their parents, except for some reason they appeared larger and more brightly colored, with a beautiful shine to their feathers. Maybe their size and bright colors were the result of the formula I feed?

The adults soon went back to nest, and the hen laid a second clutch of three eggs. This nesting did not turn out as well as the first. For about a month I had had to discontinue feeding all sprouted seeds, fruits, and vegetables. Because of an illness in the family, I did not have the time to prepare and feed the birds any extra food. None of the second clutch of Green-cheeked eggs hatched. One egg was soft-shelled; another had a thin shell; the third looked fine, but the chick did not develop and died in the egg.

During this time I found many of my other birds laid infertile eggs, and those with chicks did not feed them well. When I resumed feeding a proper diet, there was a tremendous improvement. Strong, fertile eggs were laid, and out came healthy chicks. It may be lots of extra work to feed the birds my special diet of fruits and vegetables, but I have found it is very important for breeding conures and well worth the trouble.

By now (June 1982), the Green-cheeks have nested a third and a fourth time, producing eight chicks—and they are on three eggs now.

They are still housed in the same cage, in the same flight. Once a pair of conures has nested, they are not removed from that cage. It becomes their permanent home. I do not like to disturb breeding pairs by moving them around to different cages or locations. If they are laying eggs and raising young, they'll be kept in the same place forever.

The Cactus Conure In January 1981, we purchased four Cactus Conures (*Aratinga c. cactorum*). When they were surgically sexed, it turned out that three were males and one was a hen. We let the hen choose her mate and then transferred the pair to a breeding cage in the same flight where our Green-cheeks were housed.

The next couple of months were uneventful, but on April 14, 1981, the hen laid an egg. The conures did not start to go into the nest box until about a week before the hen laid her first egg. On April 25, the clutch, a

Above: Cactus Conure, the female of the breeding pair.

Facing page: Green-cheeked Conures, *Pyrrhura molinae molinae. Top:* the breeding pair, the male facing. *Bottom:* Youngsters from the second nesting, 9 weeks old.

total of six eggs, was complete. The hen never seemed to leave the box unless I chased her out to check the eggs. Five were fertile, one was clear.

The first chick hatched on May 11, and the rest soon after, and all were doing fine. The adults were excellent parents, keeping the babies well fed. The hen left the nest box only to eat and bathe. The male was outside the box most of the time, but he spent the night inside.

The youngest baby was a week old when it looked like he

was getting a little trampled by his family. I decided to take all the chicks into the bird nursery for hand-feeding. They were so cute. Four were starting to get feathers, but the fifth was about one-third the size of the others. He may have been little, but he would stand up quite proudly, waiting for his turn to be fed.

By the time the babies were about three months old, they were eating on their own, and the youngest was just as big as the others.

We have had them surgically sexed: three hens and two

Above: The Cactus adults in their breeding cage.

Facing page: The first Cactus chicks at six weeks of age (*top*); on their weaning cage, 2 months old (*bottom*).

males. By this time (June 1982) one of the young hens has already attempted a family of her own, laying four eggs. All were infertile—more than likely the young Cactus males are not old enough to fertilize them.

The Cactus adults returned to nest again this May, laying a total of six fertile eggs. All hatched, but one chick died within a few hours. At present the other five are doing well,

growing up healthy and beautiful.

The flight containing the Cactus adults also houses a pair of their young and the pair of Green-cheeked Conures. The remaining cages in this flight are now occupied by pairs of Green-cheeked Conures *P. m. restricta*, Maroon-bellied Conures, Painted Conures, Green Conures, Barred Parakeets, and Gray-headed Lovebirds.

Peach-fronted Conures, *Aratinga aurea*, 3 months old.

Closing Thoughts

It is vitally important that aviculturists establish captive breeding programs for all species of conures. This is crucial, whether the species is rare or common.

Keep in mind that one conure was once very abundant in the United States: the Carolina Parakeet. By the late 1800s, most of these birds had been destroyed, and the species quickly became extinct. If aviculturists had collected some Carolina Parakeets, set them up for breeding, and worked with them, it is possible that these beautiful birds would be alive today in zoos and private collections. Instead, all we have left is skins in museums. If breeders work with every conure species, it can be hoped that this will never happen again. While some species may disappear from the wild, in captivity they will still be beautifully alive and enjoyed.

At the present time many species of conures are available to people in many countries. Large numbers of these birds are for sale as breeders or pets. But if the day comes when no psittacines are permitted to enter a country, or their exportation stops, even the conures most widely available now will be difficult to obtain. This is why it is very important to set up pairs of every kind of conure for breeding now, before it is too late. I know people who purchased conures for pets, then gave them a nest box. Many of these birds went to nest right in the house, in the living room.

Not many years ago, it was difficult to know if a pair of conures were indeed male and female. With advancing techniques, we can now find out for sure what sex a bird is. Now that birds can be surgically sexed by a veterinarian and paired correctly, there is no reason why anyone can't breed conures. Also, more vets are treating birds these days and doing extensive research in bird diseases. I can remember when it was difficult to find a vet who would even attempt to treat a bird for a cold.

It is truly amazing how far aviculture has progressed in the past ten years. There are literally millions of people who are now interested in keeping and breeding birds. As time passes, bird species kept in captivity usually breed and raise young more easily: budgies, lovebirds, and Cockatiels, for example. Already many conures can be bred easily: Nandays, Jandayas, and Suns. Before long, maybe all conures will breed and produce young like Cockatiels—but only if aviculturists continue to work with them.

Slender-billed Conures. Of
this adult pair, the male
shows a brighter red.

108

Subject Index

Sun Conures, 3-year-old breeding pair.

Photograph Index